BIG BIG TRAIN

WOODCUT

THE MAKING AND THE MEANING

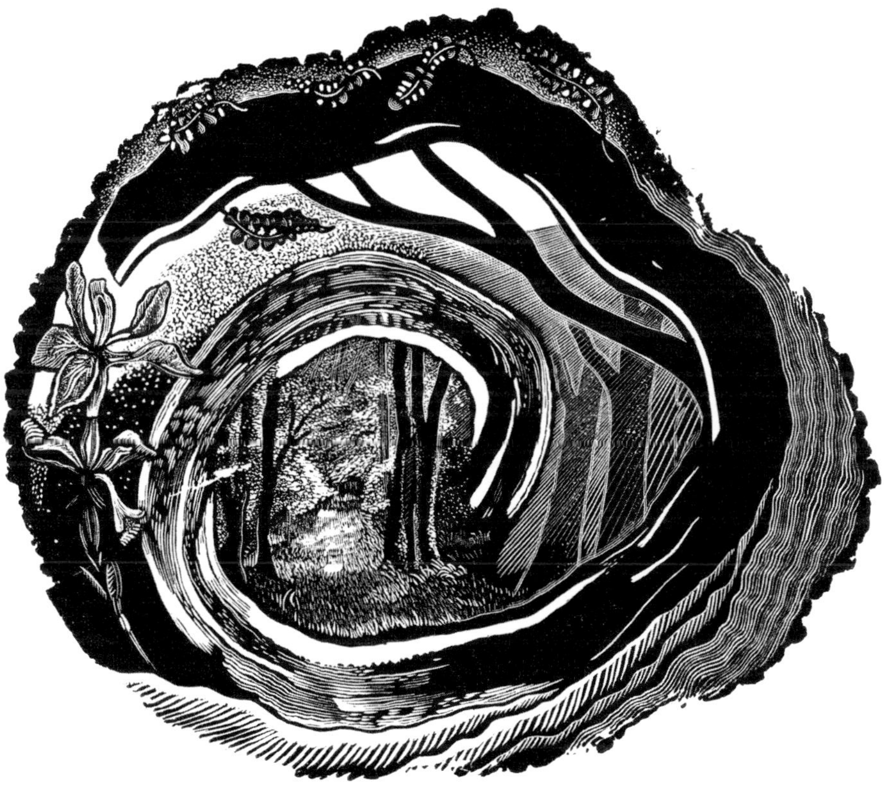

ANDY STUART

For all Passengers and those yet to board.

For Annie and Claire, with love.

And for Sue Heather. I so wish you could have heard this.

Also by Andy Stuart

A View From the Embankment, A View from the Line

The Metro Mice

KINGMAKER PUBLISHING

First published in Great Britain by Kingmaker Publishing Limited in 2026

www.kingmakerpublishing.com

ISBN 978-1-9192428-1-1

Printed in Great Britain by Biddles Books Ltd, King's Lynn, Norfolk

Contents

Let Us Begin Where It All Began

Introduction

"Plus – almost the best bit – there's acres of riveting and extremely rude sleeve notes, riddles, snaps and cartoons. A pretty thin package at times, but it still seems a real adventure. Rare, that, these days." [1]

For sure, we're here to talk about *Woodcut*, the new album by Big Big Train. But first, I want to take you back to a very different era for music. Not, as you might expect, to the early 1970s and the halcyon days of progressive rock.

No, the date I have in mind is November 1984, and the occasion is the release of Frankie Goes To Hollywood's debut album, *Welcome To The Pleasuredome*. The quote above comes from a review in *Smash Hits*, penned by editor Mark Ellen. As *Smash Hits* was the music magazine of the *zeitgeist* in Britain at the time, I imagine Ellen gave himself the privilege of writing the review because, in 1984, Frankie were as *zeitgeisty* as any artist had been since The Beatles. The arrival of their debut LP, after they'd spent most of the year crushing the charts with two of the best-selling singles of all time, was a watershed moment in the cultural life of the UK.

Therefore, it fell to writers and journalists like Ellen to describe not merely what the record contained but also – and more significantly – its meaning. Mark Ellen might not recall the details of every album review he's ever written, but his concluding remarks, particularly that closing sentence, have stayed with me ever since.

---

1 Mark Ellen, reviewing *Welcome To The Pleasuredome* in *Smash Hits*, 8-21 November 1984.

In late 1984, the release of *Welcome To The Pleasuredome* felt like the equivalent for my generation of Ziggy Stardust and the Spiders From Mars appearing on *Top Of The Pops* a decade earlier. It belonged uniquely to us in every breathless and adolescently confused detail, and the chorus of disapproval from a moralising media only fuelled our sense of rebellion. Little did we know that the record owed much to a genre of music that had supposedly been made extinct a few years earlier, notwithstanding that a reimagined Yes were at that very moment racking up triple platinum sales around the world with *90125*.

Frankie's debut album entered the citadels of teenage bedrooms across the land like some progressive rock Trojan horse, with an ex-Yes member, Trevor Horn, in charge of production and a title track utterly unlike anything else in the charts. Was it prog? At nearly 14 minutes, featuring *Close To The Edge* forest sounds and an acoustic guitar solo from Steve Howe, the song *Welcome To The Pleasuredome* could hardly be considered anything but prog. *Pleasuredome* isn't why I became a fan of the genre, but the fact that I adored (and still do) that long, sprawling epic title track does seem like a chronicle of a musical debt foretold.

But the reason I open this book about Big Big Train's *Woodcut* with an anecdote about 1980s stealth prog is because when I think about Mark Ellen's verdict (which today seems remarkably prescient in terms of nailing the significance of Frankie's *cause célèbre*), it's not the music I think about, but rather the sense of wonder and adventure that was involved in buying, owning and listening to music back then. And loath though I am to sound like my dad (who, incidentally, loathed Frankie Goes To Hollywood just as much as Mike Read[2] did), I can't help but reflect that something has been lost in the decades since.

I'm of an age to have fully embraced digital listening while still feeling a sense of nostalgia for the pre-CD era of vinyl and cassettes in which I grew up. Although it's true that you couldn't squeeze much

[2] Radio 1 DJ, Mike Read, who led the campaign for the BBC to ban Frankie's first (and gigantically successful) single, *Relax*.

additional information onto the packaging u-card of a cassette tape, the gatefold sleeve of a double or even triple album, as Ellen vividly describes, was often a garden of delights: an inspirational and tactile journey of individual exploration that you simply don't experience with digital streaming and QR code links to immersive online platforms.

While I recognise that vinyl, in relative terms, is making a comeback, CD sales have plummeted to a fraction of their former levels, so much so that the more traditional 33 rpm format is actually outselling its successor in the United States today. And all physical music formats – LP, CD, Blu-ray, DVD, and yes, even cassettes – are like a candle in a hurricane compared to the consumption of music through streaming and social media platforms. That's because the culture and infrastructure of record buying no longer exist: all those 'Championship Vinyl' record stores, their altars tended by the high priests of What May Be Considered Cool, who would issue lethal embarrassment to anyone purchasing a record they considered beneath (their) taste; college radio stations with DJs willing to play a 15 minute album track in its entirety (and then play it right over again); music magazines curated by stratospherically self-important music writers (ahem); the weekly milestone of the Top 40 countdown as the pivot point for teenage obsession. All these things have gone.

Today, the selling and buying of physical formats is mainly an esoteric niche for affluent, nostalgic music collectors, as well as enquiring younger fans who quite like the 'cool' of listening to Billie Eilish on coloured vinyl, but who wouldn't dream of purchasing a remastered copy of *Wish You Were Here*.

And who is Pink Floyd, anyway?

Didn't she do that song about getting the party started?

Of course, the contemporary viewpoint is that the party for music on physical media is very much over. It's not terribly surprising that we've arrived here, given that today you can listen to almost every song ever written and recorded for just a tenner a month, of which your favourite artist will be lucky to earn atomic fractions of a cent. The producer, musicologist and YouTube influencer Rick Beato lamented the situation in one of his recent videos:

> *"For the price of what we used to pay for one album, all the music is available on these streaming platforms, which is why music is not as valued... there is no 'sweat equity' put into obtaining it. Having it be part of your collection. Having it be part of your identity, of who you are. In the past, that was a statement. 'These are the bands I believe in, the artists that I love, that I'm going to share with my friends, and bring to school so we can hang out afterwards and listen to the album while reading the back cover and seeing who played on it.' These are things that* meant *something, and if you only have to pay $10.99 to get access to every song ever recorded, then music has basically become valueless to today's streaming audiences."*[3]

Sweat equity. I love that phrase. It evokes a time when artists played their first real six-string until their fingers bled, and no summer was complete without the rite of passage of trying to score tickets for Aerosmith (or whichever marquee artist was rolling through your local town). And the ritual of actually buying an album from a shop has become as distant and remote as an Iron Age solstice. Who else remembers saving up their pocket money and laundering piggy bank coins into the respectable grown-up currency of banknotes? Perhaps you also recall the trembling-fingered alchemy in the record shop where a month of car washes or paper rounds could be transformed into a hallowed disc of black plastic, encased in a densely illustrated sleeve of mystery and wonder? All of it has vanished. And with it has gone that sense of adventure that Mark Ellen and Rick Beato described. A new album dropping into your home screen on Spotify

---

[3] Rick Beato, *The Real Reason Music Is Getting Worse*, YouTube, June 2024.

no longer feels like an event or something that you need to plan your day around. It's just pixels.

When Big Big Train asked me to write the liner notes for *Woodcut*, I had no idea the project would develop into a book. But as I listened to the music and researched its themes and influences, it became clear that there was more to this story than just 4,000 words for a CD or LP insert. And that stirred some old-fashioned memories of the deeper imaginative involvement we enjoyed back in the day, when there was 'sweat equity' in the deal, and when we did more than simply 'consume' music.

Long-term fans already know that the finest examples of Big Big Train songwriting are not simply 'songs', but rather intelligent and thought-provoking epics that tell emotional stories set against intriguing historical or philosophical backgrounds. It's rare to find a contemporary band, in any genre, which has managed to produce such a rich body of work spanning four decades and is still discovering new and interesting things to say without sounding repetitive or suffering from diminishing creative returns.

This isn't to say that Big Big Train music is elitist or self-important, a charge that may, from time to time, have been laid at the feet of the prog rock genre; it's definitely none of those things[4]. On the contrary, what makes Big Big Train a special band is the fact that they aren't creating music as a means of showing off their intellectual or technical prowess. Their musical and lyrical reach is undeniably sophisticated and impressive, but that's simply because this is what the band does. In a culture that can often seem fixated on making the banal seem significant, it's refreshing to encounter a group of musicians whose creative DNA doesn't require artificially generated hype or FOMO to assert the value and integrity of their music.

---

[4] If you've ever been to a Big Big Train gig, and had the pleasure of chatting with the band when they come to meet up with fans after the show (*every* show), you'll know the lengths that Gregory, Nick, Rikard, Alberto, Clare, Oskar and Paul go to make themselves accessible.

So it is with *Woodcut*. It's an inspiring and profound record, with rich creative and cultural influences, virtuosic musicianship, and a stunning visual collaboration with artist and printmaker Robin Mackenzie. In short, as a concept album, it's the complete package, and one that rewards repeated listening and closer consideration of its themes and ideas.

I hope this book will help with both of those pleasures. I'm not a musicologist, nor have I tried to analyse every note and line of each song. This is a personal perspective, an extended version of those 'first reaction' videos on YouTube, rather than the definitive verdict. In the months and years ahead, I'm sure that there will be plenty of discussion about what this record 'means', as well as passionate debate about its place in the prog rock pantheon. My instinct is that Big Big Train have created a rock music classic, a true album for the ages. Perhaps we should come back and discuss for the twentieth anniversary!

Before then, where will you go as time's arrow flies? As I suggested in the abridged version of this book that serves as the liner notes, the choice is up to all of us.

However, it's a testament to the achievement of *Woodcut* that the album prompts you to even consider the question.

Rare, that, these days.

Andy Stuart
February 2026

Is this the real life, Is this just fantasy?

The magical and mysterious world of *Woodcut*

"In no other medium does one get to know an artist better than through his prints."

Ernst Ludwig Kirchner (writing as Louis de Marsalle)

Several years ago, while writing the Big Big Train tour memoir *A View From The Embankment, A View From The Line*, I interviewed Alberto Bravin about his songwriting partnership with Gregory Spawton. It was evident that despite their different backgrounds, a powerful personal and professional bond had formed between the two musicians following the untimely loss of the band's former lead singer, the inspirational David Longdon. Bravin's eyes lit up as he recalled a visit the pair made to Oslo's Munchmuseet to burn off some restless energy before Big Big Train's concert that evening.

> *"As I looked through the images and read the background notes, I turned to Greg and said, 'This is really inspiring, don't you think?' I could see he felt it too. Right there in the museum, we began exchanging ideas about how it might become a musical concept about the balance between darkness and light, the sun and the moon, the* yin *and* yang *at the heart of everything."*

Little did I realise at the time that Bravin was describing the origin story for what has evolved into Big Big Train's latest release, *Woodcut*, the band's sixteenth studio recording and – perhaps a little surprisingly – their first 'proper' concept album. The band had previously considered writing a longer, more expansive collection of music after the release of the two *English Electric* albums back in 2012 and 2013. David Longdon made some progress developing a concept that became known as *Hope,* but the project eventually lost momentum, and, in 2016, the band released *Folklore* instead.

The years passed, during which there never seemed to be a right time to go all in on a career-defining prog saga. The pandemic, personnel changes and the tragedy of Longdon's untimely passing each presented their own commercial and artistic challenges. With hindsight, it seems evident that a Big Big Train concept album could have seemed almost like an indulgence rather than a logical creative next step. This could explain why, even in 2024, Big Big Train manager Nick Shilton seemed dubious about following the most well-worn path in prog, a point acknowledged by Gregory Spawton in a blog post when *Woodcut* was announced.

> *"The not-exactly-overwhelmingly-positive-feedback to the idea of BBT working on a concept album is probably explained by the long dark shadows cast by Yes'* Tales From Topographic Oceans *and Genesis'* The Lamb Lies Down On Broadway. *The former is one of those albums that will always be associated with the idea that prog rock is inherently pretentious (and therefore possibly a bit crap) whilst the latter is the album that brought to an end the Peter Gabriel era of Genesis (and did so in an anti-climactic way, with the last show of the* Lamb *tour being cancelled due to poor ticket sales)."*[5]

In fairness to Spawton, he quickly adds that although this was once considered conventional wisdom, today's prog fans are more likely to regard both albums as classics of the genre, citing *Tales From Topographic Oceans* as Rikard Sjöblom's favourite Yes album, no less. I

[5] *'Oh God, not a concept album...'* by Gregory Spawton on Substack, 11 November 2025.

certainly wouldn't dispute the opinion of such a talented musician as Big Big Train's Swedish guitarist. However, I must admit that side 3 of *Topographic Oceans* still feels a bit like an Ishihara test, whose patterns stubbornly refuse to appear, no matter how hard I try to see them. But in a world where even mainstream artists are exploring the creative potential of the concept album—and you can hardly be more mainstream than Taylor Swift's *Life Of A Showgirl*—perhaps the world is ready for Big Big Train's first full venture into the genre.

Today, Gregory Spawton's memory of his and Bravin's visit to the Munchmuseet is still very fresh.

> *"We were wandering through the gallery, reading about the technique of creating a woodcut, which is an illustration technique where the artist makes a positive illustration out of a negative original. There was already an undercurrent of something mysterious in the room, which was shadowy and dimly lit to preserve the fragile prints. I remember catching a gleam in Alberto's eyes as we gazed at one particular woodcut. It was as if we had the same thought simultaneously, like there's something here, some idea just waiting to be brought to life. We left the museum buzzing, little realising how much the concept was going to take over our lives for the next few years."*

But the rest of the band were soon in the know, as Clare Lindley confirms.

> *"One of the benefits of being all together on a tour bus is that even though you're focused on the shows, you have a lot of time to throw ideas around regarding future projects. We'd said on more than one occasion,* 'You know what, we've never done a big narrative concept album,' *so when Greg and Alby started talking about* Woodcut *– not the full story* per se *but the general idea and the title – it felt like serendipity, as if something had fallen into our laps that was just meant to be."*

> *"And I like working with a title as an anchor for a song,"* says Spawton. *"Because it can lead you in a certain direction, and here, the title* Woodcut *naturally pointed the way for the entire album. Alberto and I both liked the word 'woodcut'. It can signify both the creative process and the thing being created, so there's a double meaning there."*

This was in September 2023, and the band has covered plenty of ground across Europe, the United States and Canada since then, but I believe fans will feel that the wait has been more than worth it. *Woodcut* is easily Big Big Train's most ambitious musical project to date. Whereas on previous albums, echoes of melody would reappear as motifs in other songs – as on *English Electric*'s *The First Rebreather* and *The Permanent Way*, or the wistful 'shallow enders' refrain that links *Beneath The Masts* and *Last Eleven* on 2024's *The Likes Of Us* – here, the abundance of themes and ideas forms one complete piece of music, elaborately stitched together with remarkable attention to detail. The final mix, for example, has more than 400 individual tracks. And while that could have resulted in an album that was a little too clever, a little too crafted, ultimately *Woodcut* is a spectacularly emotional, passionate and, above all, human *tour de force*.

Much of the credit for this, as Gregory Spawton and Clare Lindley are quick to point out, is due to Alberto Bravin, as the arranger-in-chief for all the ideas that the band gathered together following the release of *The Likes Of Us* in March 2024.

> *"I've always said that songwriting is a messy business,"* says Spawton. *"But Alberto threw himself into the task of picking through all the material and figuring out what might work – sometimes with a change of key here, or moving something from major to minor there – as a single piece of music."*

Clare Lindley agrees.

> *"People are working away on their own pieces of music all the time. So, when it comes to gathering material for the next record, there*

will naturally be ideas that people can put forward and say, 'Well, I've got this thing that could maybe fit as a song, or as a section for a longer track.' But Alberto was the mastermind, the one who had the sense of how the whole album would come together."

"I think we all felt very strongly that somebody had to take the lead to organise the musical side of things," continues Spawton. *"What was different with* Woodcut *is that once you decide 'We're going to do a concept album', having a Dropbox folder filled with lots of different snippets isn't necessarily helpful, because when you're telling a story through music, you need your themes and ideas to be consistent. And honestly, it's genius what he's been able to do in terms of taking all those little strands and weaving them together. It's not simply a question of assembling a musical jigsaw; it requires exceptional compositional skills. The outstanding contemporary example is probably Neal Morse, but I think Alberto's achievement is right up there with the best."*

Bravin himself cites an almost obsessive attention to detail, combined with a wariness of presenting unfinished ideas, as the impetus behind his approach.

"I know that perfection is the enemy of the good, but with Woodcut*, I almost didn't want people to hear anything until I had one continuous piece of music ready to share. The thing about a band is that it's like a family, so sometimes it can be difficult for everyone to agree. It's a lot easier to reach an understanding if the original idea is really well thought through.*

"Assembling the initial demo was a mountain of work, and it came at a time when we were also mixing Are We Nearly There Yet? *I think I spent a solid three to four months sifting through the band's contributions, cleaning them up, adjusting keys so tracks would flow into each other, writing new melodies and vocal lines, moving sections around and adding themes from other songs. I had*

a project in Logic called 'A.B. Chaos' because that's kind of what it was like! I had a clear idea in my head of how it would ultimately sound, but to reach that point using so many different elements was the most intense thing I've ever done. And it was all because I wanted that first full demo to be the best possible expression of how I viewed the concept."

The sacrifices were definitely worth it, however, even if the patience and curiosity of other band members were sometimes stretched.

> *"I knew Alby was working long hours to pull everything together, and he knows I am not the most patient of people,"* acknowledges Gregory Spawton. *"He had to fend off my constant requests for updates while I had to learn to sit on my hands and wait for the alchemy to happen!"*

And although Bravin laboured intensively over his initial demo, the rest of his bandmates still found plenty of room for inspiration when it came to recording their individual parts, as Oskar Holldorff explains.

> *"I could really relate to what Alberto did because, although I'm focused on keyboards with Big Big Train, in my other band, Dim Gray, I have a similar 'producer' role. I know from experience that sometimes you have to avoid falling in love with that initial mix too much, because then you limit your ability to imagine it differently. And that can be difficult when you have someone like Alberto who can produce these incredibly polished demos.*
>
> *"But when I first heard that original demo, I was very excited because I felt there would be plenty of opportunity for the rest of us to fill in the finer details. I think we all felt we'd been given these wonderful building blocks of music that we could turn into something more intricate. You could see the big picture. The challenge for the band was to ensure that each song had its own identity and reason to exist. In other words, to make sure that it*

didn't just sound like a copy-and-paste – 'Here's that riff you heard earlier, but nothing has really changed' – kind of thing. And I think we've achieved that on Woodcut.*"*

With Bravin's master demo in place, in April 2025 the band reassembled at Sweetwater Studios in Fort Wayne, Indiana, following their North American shows and Cruise To The Edge. Rikard Sjöblom remembers it being a crowded, but enjoyable, schedule.

"It was great to spend time together in the studio, just like we did in Trieste with The Likes Of Us. *The main aim at Sweetwater was to lay down all the rhythm tracks with Greg and NDV, but I had a lot of fun accompanying them, and I was also able to record all my guitar parts. I'd go in and sit with Rob [Aubrey, engineer] or Alby and whoever else was in the booth at the time. There'd be moments when Greg would listen in, and he'd give me a thumbs-up if something sounded good. I really enjoy that kind of instant feedback, because when I'm recording alone in my home studio, I can be quite hard on myself, and I start to second-guess whether the rest of the band will like what I'm doing. It saves a lot of back and forth and stress when we can be together."*

"For a musician, recording at Sweetwater was like being a child let loose in a sweetshop," says Oskar Holldorff. *"We had access to an almost absurd amount of equipment - just about every kind of instrument and amp you might ever wish to play. For me, that meant being able to use a beautiful Yamaha CX7 grand piano and having a variety of keyboards on hand, including an immaculate Fender Rhodes, a Wurlitzer, and an original Hammond B3 organ. Although I recorded some extra synth pieces once I returned to my home studio, for the most part, all the piano and keyboard sounds were captured during our stay in Fort Wayne."*

Although Alberto Bravin was the mastermind on the musical side of the project, the other foundational strength of the album is the storyline that Gregory Spawton and Clare Lindley developed from the original spark that gripped the imaginations of Spawton and Bravin that fateful morning in Oslo.

Lyrically, *Woodcut* is a dark, supernatural fable about a troubled illustrator frustrated by his failure to find creative fulfilment and ravaged by doubts about the value of his lifetime of sacrifice. The story is told through a series of poetic and often haunting lyrics, which are notable for their shifting moods and moments of penetrating psychological insight. In vinyl form, the album neatly divides into four relatively self-contained movements that describe The Artist's journey in a loosely structured way. But even when listened to as a complete piece of music, the different songs, per Oskar Holldorff's comments, feel pleasingly distinct and varied.

Following the overture, *Inkwell Black*, the story begins with an introduction to the troubled character, whose mental trauma serves as the driving force behind the narrative. In *The Artist*, we are quickly introduced to an emotional disturbance that is threatening to undermine every creative impulse. Clare Lindley has written a beautifully concise and quite heart-breaking reflection on the isolating and sometimes obsessive nature of artistic ambition:

Searching for perfection
But second-guessing everything
To carve a thousand birds
And never hear them sing

The original impulse to create art – or at least, the art that truly matters – is not about fame or glory, but mostly stems from a deeply felt need for self-expression. The absence of this fulfilment has left The Artist in a vulnerable and challenging place. So, what do we often do when the pressure of life seems overwhelming? We try to take stock and gain a clearer view of *The Lie Of The Land*. Seeking a fresh perspective and renewed purpose in the calming influence of nature, The Artist wanders deep into a forest where he stumbles across a piece of ancient heartwood. This discovery seems to dislodge his mental barriers and unleash an exultant, almost reckless, surge of creativity.

Light finds its way through the trees
It's all I was searching for

But as he begins carving into the heartwood using *The Sharpest Blade*, The Artist is aware of a mysterious presence that seems to guide his hand with almost inhuman confidence and precision. Perhaps a more grounded individual would have paid heed to this feeling of unease, to the 'lie' of the land being revealed, but even though he is fearful of the traumas he may be drawing upon for inspiration, The Artist is too far gone to set aside his tools.

When the first print of the woodcut is finally realised using the *Albion Press*, The Artist is transported into a sublime natural world that is nothing less than his illustration brought to life. As the walls, both physical and mental, dissolve, this wondrous *Arcadia* has a vivid, almost supernatural beauty, like the first morning of the world.

A world that feels so perfect
How could it ever be a dream?

But as the vision fades, The Artist is abruptly exiled. And the more he fights to reconstruct the *Warp And Weft* of this paradise, the more he seems to be unpicking the threads of his own sanity.

Time stops - how I can't explain
Dig in - the more I go, the less of me remains

Belatedly, he realises that the deep-rooted feelings and experiences that gave rise to Arcadia are a *Chimaera* and much darker than they first appeared. Indeed, his mental pathways and private emotional landmarks seem to be augmented by others he doesn't recognise, leading him to question who else may have been brought to the *Dead Point* of their deepest desires.

Whose footsteps made the paths I follow?
Who has tamed the places I have found?

No longer able to trust in what may be real and truthful, The Artist tries to escape, but the supernatural forces won't allow him to *Cut And Run*. And as the album reaches its climax, we sense his hold on life may be fading. The eldritch scent of *Hawthorn White* implies he is drifting towards the cosmic, *Counting Stars* as he reflects on the meaning of his life and his place in the universe. As The Artist makes his *Last Stand*, the outcome – and by implication, his soul – hangs in the balance. What force will prevail in this battle between the forces of darkness and light?

The woodcut technique, which captivated Gregory Spawton and Alberto Bravin in Oslo, is one of the oldest illustrative methods, dating back to ancient China and gaining prominence in Europe during the Middle Ages. It's a relief printing process, meaning the design is carved into the surface of a wooden block, traditionally a hardwood like boxwood, which holds fine detail well. Artists use gouges, knives and chisels to carefully cut away the areas they do not want to print. The raised and uncarved areas are then inked and pressed onto paper to produce an image. While often associated with bold lines and high contrast, skilled artists and wood carvers can achieve remarkable degrees of detail and expression. Modern woodcut endures as both a fine art form and a historical printmaking technique, admired for its tactile quality, physicality and visual impact.

Initially used to imprint textiles, the use of woodcut became more prominent from the 15th century when the technology for making paper migrated westward from India and China into Europe. In the digital era, it's hard to appreciate the far-reaching social, economic and cultural impact of being able to produce paper in almost limitless quantities. Arriving at roughly the same moment as Johannes Gutenberg's printing press, the transformation of paper from a costly, handcrafted item to an affordable, convenient and accessible medium must have felt almost alchemical, and represented one of the most dazzling conjunctions in human history.

By enabling the transfer of information across vast periods of time and distance, the humble printed page became a catalyst for modernising civilisation, a means of disseminating political, scientific and intellectual ideas, and, crucially, artistic inspiration. Paper would redefine the entire world by revolutionising the means by which people understood it. In every respect, it was an ingenious device that liberated 'poets, painters, writers and dreamers'[6], allowing their ideas and visions to influence and be seen by exponentially greater numbers of people.

During the Middle Ages, woodcuts were most commonly used as illustrations for the surge of printed books that emerged following the invention of the Gutenberg press in 1440. This was because the lightweight, portable characteristics of the carved blocks gave printers more flexibility during the book production process. "One of the great advantages of woodcuts is that the blocks could be

[6] A phrase from the lyric of the Big Big Train song *A Mead Hall In Winter.*

placed in the same framework as movable type and printed in the same press," explains Wendy Thompson of the Metropolitan Museum of New York[7]. By 1500, the volume of books being produced by presses throughout Europe had already reached 20 million copies, and during the next century, that figure would increase tenfold. Woodcuts were frequently reused by different printers because good designs were expensive and difficult to produce. For example, carvings used by William Caxton in his 1483 edition of Chaucer's *The Canterbury Tales* were still being used for future editions some 50 years later.

The convergence of commercial book manufacturing with the artistic potential of woodcut propelled the medium into new realms of imaginative possibility. Before book printing became widespread, early woodcuts tended towards thick outlines with minimal shading. This was because the fragility of overly fine lines caused the carved blocks to collapse when subjected to the pressure of the press. And, of course, they were mostly carved to create black and white prints which favoured bolder and simpler designs.

However, the increasingly sophisticated demands of the industry drove European illustrators to produce ever more intricate artwork, arguably none more so than the German artist Albrecht Dürer, who elevated the medium to unprecedented levels of technical expertise. Dürer's woodcut, *Samson Rending the Lion*, featured such masterful gradations of tone and texture – particularly the remarkable tapered lines of the lion's mane – that a fellow contemporary artist, Erasmus of Rotterdam,

7 *Woodcut Book Illustration in Renaissance Italy: The First Illustrated Books*, by Wendy Thompson, Metropolitan Museum of New York, 2004.

suggested adding colour would be a negative act that "would do injury to the work".

Elsewhere, however, Renaissance craftsmen *did* begin to introduce colour, allowing them to emulate the *chiaroscuro* effect in painting, where strong contrasts between light and dark create a sense of three-dimensional space within the flat image. Illustrators could achieve these effects by using multiple blocks for each colour tone to suggest degrees of shading, leaving the cutaway parts, which remained white on the paper, to act as the highlights.

One of the great masterpieces of *chiaroscuro* woodcut is Hans Baldung Grien's eerie *Scene of Witchcraft* (1510). Set in a clearing among blasted trees, it depicts three witches ascending into the night sky, their figures wrapped in coils of steam and illuminated by flickering highlights that sharply contrast with the surrounding darkness. Printers would sometimes use an orange-brown tone combination to reproduce the illustration, casting a hellish glow over the scene, which, for medieval audiences, must have seemed truly out of this world.

However, after this halcyon period, the technique of woodcut began to fade out of fashion during the 16th century, as *intaglio* printing, where the image is cut into a metal plate[8] rather than a wooden block, became the preferred method for book illustration. Besides the durability of the metal, the use of *intaglio* techniques expanded the range of visual devices that artists could employ, such as cross-hatching and deep-swelling lines, which enabled them to create a wider variety of tones and contrasts in their images. Because engravings, etchings[9] and type required different printing methods, illustrations produced using

---

[8] Typically copper, hence 'copperplate' script.

[9] A note on the difference between an etching and an engraving: Both are *intaglio* techniques, but an engraving (sometimes called copperplate engraving) is where the artist cuts grooves directly into the metal using a tool known as a 'burin'. An etching, in contrast, is created by covering the plate with an acid resistant resin, or 'ground', and using a needle to pick through the ground and score a design onto the metal surface below. When the plate is covered with acid, the chemical bites into the surface to etch out the design, while areas that are covered by the ground remain unaffected. Engraving will make a much deeper incision than etching, which leaves smoother, more superficial marks. As a consequence, etching takes far less time and became the preferred method for commercial book makers during the period.

intaglio methods were printed onto separate sheets, which meant it was no longer possible to set image and text on a single, integrated page. Between the 1500s and the early 1800s, *intaglio* became the dominant method for printing images using commercial presses in Europe.

In the Far East, it was a different story. This was the halcyon period for Japanese woodcut printing, a style that became known as *ukiyo-e*. The term *ukiyo-e* (浮世絵) literally means "picture of the floating world", although in Japanese culture of the time, the evocative phrase 'floating world' actually referred to the hedonistic entertainment to be found in the licensed brothels and theatres of major Japanese cities, and illustrations would depict *geiko*, courtesans and Kabuki actors who were both low in social status and yet, through *ukiyo-e*, also the style icons of their era.

Ukiyo-e differed from European woodcut illustrations because it was a handcrafted medium that eschewed mechanical presses. Hand printing allowed greater control over colour and contrast than machine printing. Labour was typically divided between the artist who drew the source image, the carver who developed the woodblocks for printing and the printer who made the impression of the block onto paper. Although *ukiyo-e* has a rich and varied history, it is perhaps best known in the West for the illustrations of Kitagawa Utamaro, Tōshūsai Sharaku and, in particular, Katsushika Hokusai, whose 1831 print, *The Great Wave off Kanagawa*, is one of the most famous illustrations in world art. What distinguished *ukiyo-e* from earlier European woodcut methods was the full-colour *nishiki-e* prints made from multiple woodblocks, each block used for a different colour. In Japanese, *nishiki* means 'brocade' and the term was used because the richly coloured prints produced by this method resembled ornate brocade fabric, an effect further enhanced by sophisticated embossing and gradation techniques at the end of the Edo period (1603-1868).

Just as the engraved illustrations of Hablot Knight Browne were sensationally successful in Victorian England, accompanying the serialised novels of Charles Dickens, so, too, were *nishiki-e* in contemporary Japanese society. According to the Hoover Institution Library & Archives, "8,000 copies were printed for one set of blockbuster *nishiki-e* in a single month in the late 1840s... *nishiki-e* were commercial products spearheaded by profit-minded publishers who hired teams of artists, carvers, and printers to collaborate on print series based on broad themes or one-off designs."[10]

And this was just for one image within a thriving industry. Japanese art experts estimate that the annual production of *ukiyo-e* illustrations in a typical year in the 1850s was 4 to 5 million sheets.

It was an English wood engraver from the rural north-east of England who revived the popularity of the woodcut in western Europe in the late 18th century. Thomas Bewick's interest in country life and nature could easily have made him the hero of a Big Big Train song. He grew up in the bucolic surroundings of a farm in Northumberland, and as a child, in a biographical detail that almost reads like a line from a Gregory Spawton lyric, used a pin to draw sketches of animals and birds in the corner of his Sunday hymn book.

Bewick's great insight was to pioneer a method of carving into wood that rivalled the fine detail of metal engraving. He achieved this breakthrough by using blocks of hardwood, such as box or maple, which had been cut across the grain rather than along it. Prepared in this way, the wood was more durable and better able to withstand the fine cutting techniques needed for highly detailed images.

The only drawback was that working with the end grain limited the size of the block, so most of Thomas Bewick's illustrations are miniature marvels no larger than a few inches square. But his innovative craftsmanship allowed Bewick to work the wood with a metalworker's burin, creating delicate incisions comparable to those seen in *intaglio* illustrations. Freed from the constraints of traditional woodcut methods, Bewick could vary the depth of his cuts and create contrasting sections printed in lighter and darker shades of grey, which in turn allowed for much greater depth in his images.

---

10 *Nishiki-e Defined: A Core Topic of Modern Japan*, The Hoover Institution Library & Archives.

In England, the 19th century revival of woodcut art probably reached its zenith in 1896 with the publication of the *Kelmscott Chaucer*, a remarkable collaboration between the celebrated designer William Morris, the fine artist Edward Burne-Jones[11] and the wood engraver William Hooper. Like Thomas Bewick's childhood, the story of the *Kelmscott Chaucer* is a tale that you could easily imagine as the inspiration for a lost track from Big Big Train's *English Electric* albums.

Morris founded the Kelmscott Press as the Victorian era was drawing to a close to uphold his personal belief in the value of books as beautiful objects in themselves. His goal of producing richly illustrated volumes using traditional methods revealed a deep reverence for medieval craftsmanship and design. Morris himself prepared the lavish, fairy-tale illuminated borders and frames for the Chaucer edition, Edward Burne-Jones created no fewer than 87 illustrations, and the designs of both artists were then committed to woodblocks by William Hooper. However, Hooper fell out with the aesthete Morris by refusing to recognise the inherent artistry involved in reproducing such sensuous and densely detailed designs. Unlike in Japanese *ukiyo-e*, it seems there was far less sense of teamwork and interdependence between designer, artist and carver.

According to Simon Cooke:

> *"Hooper was a self-proclaimed Socialist and seemed to relish his status as a highly-skilled artisan. However, it is interesting to note that he actively opposed John Ruskin's idea that the craftsman should be an active participant or co-author in the production of fine art"*, insisting that the carver *"should be no more than a technical medium, capturing the artist's 'character and feeling' and making sure to 'sacrifice his own individuality'."*[12]

---

11 Geoff Parks points out that works by Morris and Burne-Jones may be admired in the Chapel of Jesus College, Cambridge, where some of the scenes for Big Big Train's *Merry Christmas* video were filmed and the vocal contributions of the choristers to the song were recorded.

12 *Hooper and Wood-Engraving as a Craft*, Simon Cooke for *The Victorian Web*, 2017.

Perhaps this disconnect explains why, despite its extravagant beauty, there's a certain sterility about the *Kelmscott Chaucer*. As Simon Cooke notes, a total of 438 copies of the book were printed over two years: 13 on vellum and 425 on handmade paper. 48 paper editions were specially bound in white pigskin, featuring a design created by William Morris himself. The whole enterprise feels weirdly similar to some lavish, limited edition rock music box set, where the attention to presentation and packaging luxury almost loses sight of the fact that this was once just an album, bought by nerdy teenagers who'd saved up their paper round money or sold off their elder brother's record collection to solicit funds for their own.[13]

Even in the triumphant moment of publishing the *Kelmscott Chaucer*, Morris lamented what he perceived as the lifeless, almost mechanical, aspect of Hooper's work. Morris had aspired to the rich sensuality and emotive force of 15th century craftsmen, but in criticising Hooper, he had clearly failed to appreciate that simply copying their methods would never allow him to recreate the feelings that the medieval artisans had tried to express through their art. Post-Industrial Revolution society, which – whether they liked it or not – also included aesthetes like Morris, John Ruskin and Walter Pater, was on the wrong side of the epoch. You could revere the past, but you could never hope to return to it just by reviving illuminated manuscripts.[14]

[13] One of my classmates at school literally did this, which is how I came to obtain a pretty immaculate copy of *Yessongs* for the princely sum of £2. Soon afterwards, the family moved away and my classmate left the school. Well, that was the official story, at least, but since big brother is always watching there may have been other forces involved!

[14] It does pose an interesting parallel question, which there isn't time to fully discuss here, about the relationship between the original progressive rock pioneers and those who follow them in the 21st century. Isn't what modern bands are doing with prog similar to what William Morris was trying to achieve with the *Kelmscott Chaucer*? This, of course, is also the same criticism levelled with even greater force at generative AI – i.e. that it's purely derivative. In the case of AI, we'll come on to that in due course, but as far as derivation in prog is concerned, I think it's less clear cut. In my mind, William Morris was incapable of conceiving any kind of illustration that wasn't strictly prescribed by the medieval forms that he admired. In comparison, I would argue that the best modern prog bands, like Big Big Train, aren't replicating old ideas so much as using them as a springboard to take the genre forward into new and unexplored areas. Classic prog might be the starting point, but it's not the final destination.

To express emotions that were relevant and contemporary in a world of steam engines, wireless cables and electricity, the techniques of woodcut would also need to reflect progress rather than bourgeois nostalgia. It feels significant, therefore, that as Morris was preparing to publish the first edition of his neo-medieval tome, Edvard Munch was unveiling his Symbolist masterpiece, *The Scream*, at a gallery in Oslo. Telling because it was Munch, not Morris, nor the other reverential medievalists in the Pre-Raphaelite movement, who was turned on and tuned in to the wavelength of the new era.

It's fortunate that Alberto Bravin and Gregory Spawton were killing time in the Munchmuseet in Oslo rather than London's Victoria & Albert Museum on that damp August morning in 2023. I can't imagine them being similarly inspired to create a concept album by the intricate designs of luxury curtains. Munch, on the other hand, was a true progressive in every sense of the word. And like all good prog artists, he was pushing the boundaries with work that sharply divided popular opinion and took him light years away from what contemporaries like William Morris were doing, as art critic Waldemar Januszczak remarks:

> *"Munch's art wasn't just responding to another drumbeat. It was from another planet. Look closely into any picture and you will see paint doing things that no one had ever previously asked of it."*[15]

Replace the words "picture" and "paint" with "album" and "music", and you could be talking about some of the startling achievements of

[15] *'Edvard Munch at the Courtauld: the tortured genius who craved the sun'*, Waldemar Januszczak, June 2022.

the early prog pioneers. Back in the day, reviewers spoke in similar terms about *Close To The Edge.*

> *"Well, if there's a problem involved in placing or defining Yes' music, it's a direct result of our establishing rigid criteria and admitting only that which qualifies, rather than expanding our own borders of perception in accordance with what artists choose to present."*[16]

And here is Bill Bruford, who played drums on that record, talking even more directly about the first time he saw fellow prog act, King Crimson, at the Speakeasy in 1969:

> *"And then, this God Almighty powerful beast uncoiled itself. It wasn't at all like anything else anybody had ever heard. Nobody knew what the hell this thing was. The lyrics were different, the way the musicians conducted themselves was different, the sound was different, there was a strobe light making an extremely kind of hard-edged [scene] — it just kind of froze everybody."*[17]

Of course, Bruford was so inspired by what he heard that night that he eventually left Yes to take up drumming duties in the very band that had arrested everyone's attention at the Speakeasy. In this regard, for prog rock fans to regard Munch's brilliance as a kindred ancestor doesn't feel like too much of a stretch. And while some 19th century onlookers found the anguish in paintings like *The Scream* too intense and disturbing, for the majority, it was the intensity that made the painting so otherworldly, so compelling and so forward-looking. While William Morris and his admirers wanted to turn the clock back to bygone eras, the work of Edvard Munch and other Symbolist artists hurtled you into an unsettling and unpredictable future. The great conflict of 1914-1918 was less than 20 years away, the point at which the old and new orders would be slammed together in the chaos of

16 Review of *Close To The Edge* by Richard Cromelin, *Rolling Stone*, 9 November 1972.

17 King Crimson's *21st Century Schizoid Man*: Inside Prog's Big Bang, *Rolling Stone*, 1 October 2019.

industrialised warfare. Comparing those two works from the mid-1890s, *The Scream* and the *Kelmscott Chaucer*, it's the radicalism of Munch's agonised individual that seems more representative of the world-in-waiting than the fastidious designs of Morris and Burne-Jones.

Despite the reputation of both artwork and artist, Munch's *The Scream* isn't a cry for help from someone feeling lonely and adrift in urban society. Instead, it expresses the deeper horror of being the only person able to hear the universe howl. Such psychological torment can be viewed as a vivid metaphor for mental illness, or at least the burden of possessing a singular vision that no one else can share or even understand. This aspect certainly feels relevant to the main character and the song *The Artist* on *Woodcut*.

Munch's ability to visualise his deeply personal neuroses and feelings of unease helped catapult art into the 20th century and would later make him a superstar. His most famous work is part of the vocabulary of the Internet thanks to having its own emoji – the face that launched a billion clips[18] – and successive generations of artists have continued to draw inspiration from his work. Earlier, I mentioned how Munch turned on and tuned in to his surroundings. To anyone attempting to use creativity to make sense of the late 1960s and early 1970s, what else could the vivid, lysergic swirls of *The Scream* have looked like if not the perfect depiction of a bad trip? Munch wrote of his inspiration:

> *"I was walking down the road with two friends when the sun set; suddenly, the sky turned as red as blood. I stopped and leaned against the fence, feeling unspeakably tired. Tongues of fire and blood stretched over the bluish-black fjord. My friends went on walking, while I lagged behind, shivering with fear. Then I heard the enormous, infinite scream of nature."*

[18] No one publishes formal metrics for individual emojis, but according to the emojitracker website, *Face Screaming In Fear* is the 53rd most popular icon, meaning its usage may be close to 4 billion instances per year such is the volume of posts and messages.

That feverish tone and feeling of acute alienation and bewilderment is as visceral as the ravings of Dennis Hopper's paranoid photojournalist in Francis Ford Coppola's Vietnam War epic, *Apocalypse Now.*

> *"This is the way the fucking world ends! Look at this fucking shit we're in, man! Not with a bang, but with a whimper. And with a whimper, I'm fucking splitting, Jack."*

Hopper's wide-eyed fear is exactly what we see in *The Scream*: a person who appears to be literally splitting apart before our eyes. In 1971, at the height of the Vietnam War, John Lennon had sung:

One thing you can't hide
Is when you're crippled inside

We now realise that the trauma of trying to keep up appearances, pretending that nothing is happening, can be the eye of the storm before the mental hurricane tears everything down. Coppola's haunting and visionary movie revolves around the madness of a single, mythical individual, Colonel Kurtz, who has been driven insane by trying to fulfil a military command that makes no sense whatsoever, and who creates hell on earth in the vacuum left behind by the disintegration of his personality. In the early 1970s, the Vietnam War became a potent symbol of the dark heart of human nature and how it inevitably corrupts any and every noble ideal. And that symbol had already proven inspirational for progressive artists and musicians.

Decades after Munch revealed his unsettlingly weird painting, you can easily see his influence on one of the most famous album covers in prog rock, Barry Godber's primal 'Schizoid Man' illustration for King Crimson's *In The Court Of The Crimson King*, released in October 1969. The title song from the album, with Peter Sinfield's furious lyrical criticisms of Vietnam-era politics and the industrial-military complex, expressed the seething fears of his contemporaries. "Everything multi-tracked a billion times, and when you listen, you get a billion times the impact," wrote The Who's Pete Townshend for a King Crimson promo pack – and he was a man who knew a thing or two about being a spokesman for a generation.

> "*It was constant,*" said Peter Sinfield in a 2019 interview[19]. "*Pictures of the bombers over Cambodia, dropping sticks and sticks of bombs on the poor peasants underneath, and there was that picture of the little girl running down the road on fire. I wanted [our music] to frighten people and upset them and scare them and [make them] run out the door.*"

In many ways, Vietnam, the first televisual war, was the modern manifestation of the universe screaming, just as Edvard Munch had sensed 80 years earlier, because it seemed total and relentless, streamed in vivid colour night after night on the evening news. Now, everyone was screaming. And some might say that we've never stopped since.

Munch began creating woodcut illustrations in 1895, the same year that *The Scream* went on display in Oslo, and a year before Morris, Burne-Jones and Hooper published their woodcut edition of Chaucer. The same groundbreaking and troubled mindset that inspired Munch's painting is also evident in his printing methods, which drew on influences from around the globe.

Japanese culture became very popular in Scandinavia in the 1880s and 1890s as Japan turned westward through increased trade, leading to an influx of oriental art and design into Europe, the so-called 'Japonisme' movement. The Danish artist and art critic Karl Madsen published a book called *Japansk Malerkunst* (Japanese Painting) in 1885, which was influential as the first authoritative work on the subject in a Nordic language. Vincent van Gogh, who Munch greatly admired, was inspired by Utagawa Hiroshige's Japanese woodblock print, *The Plum Garden at Kameido*, and created an oil painting copy in 1887 titled *Flowering Plum Orchard (after Hiroshige)*. According to modern Dutch

---

[19] King Crimson's *21st Century Schizoid Man*: Inside Prog's Big Bang, Rolling Stone, 1 October 2019.

artist and curator Zen Dageraad Visser, Japonisme arrived at a pivotal moment because Western art had reached a crossroads:

> *"The advent of photography in the mid-19th century fundamentally challenged the need for painting to be purely representational. If a camera could capture reality with perfect accuracy, what was the painter's role? Academic traditions felt stale to many, bound by rigid rules of perspective, anatomy, and historical subjects. Artists were seeking new ways to express modernity, emotion, and subjective experience, moving beyond strict mimesis (the imitation of reality).* Ukiyo-e *offered a completely different paradigm. It wasn't about perfect anatomical accuracy or illusionistic depth. It was about capturing the essence of a scene or person with graphic strength and decorative beauty. Its focus on line, flat color, and dynamic composition provided a ready-made visual language for artists looking to break free from the constraints of realism and academic rules. This resonated deeply with artists who wanted to explore the expressive potential of color, line, and form for their own sake, rather than solely in service of representation."*[20]

Munch was influenced by studying Post-Impressionists like van Gogh, Paul Gauguin and Henri de Toulouse-Lautrec, and incorporated much of their style and technique into his own work. What particularly impressed him was their rejection of literal realism in favour of depicting the world through personal emotional experience and imagination, as Dageraad Visser describes. This new visual language allowed Munch to "imagine the inside out" and reveal his (and our) most raw private emotions. Munch's friend, the German-Polish writer and anarchist Stanislaw Przybyszewski, described him as a 'painter of the soul' who:

---

[20] *How Japanese Woodblock Prints Blew the Minds of Western Artists (And Changed Everything)* by Zen Dageraad Visser.

> *"attempts to depict phenomena of the soul spontaneously through colour. He paints in a manner that only a naked individuality can do, and sees with eyes that have turned away from the world of reality towards an inner world."*

It's perhaps no coincidence that this psychoanalytical approach to painting and illustration aligned with Freud's development of psychoanalytical theory, which emerged in the 1890s. Munch's paintings and prints serve almost as a visual premonition of Freudian ideas relating to anxiety, repression, jealousy, and the unconscious.

The Norwegian quickly mastered the ancient techniques of woodcut before exploding the boundaries of the medium with his revolutionary 'jigsaw' method of printmaking. This involved cutting a single woodblock into pieces, allowing him to ink separate parts of the image in different colours and intensities, and enabling intricate layering effects. He then reassembled these pieces to make the final print. Today, Munch's coloured blocks resemble the exploded fragments of life bursting out of a Roger Dean painting, seeds of life for an entirely new visual universe.

Using woodcut, Munch was able to transcend surfaces and bring relief to the underlying instability he perceived in the world. If woodcut is a medium that obliges the artist to reveal "the light trapped by the darkness", then it was ideally suited to the Norwegian artist's troubled sensibility. Brilliant though he was, Munch was prone to dark moods and chronic insecurity throughout his adult life. Today, we are more familiar with the destructive potential of creative genius and what can happen when private talent is floated on the stock market of public acclaim. But like Amy besieged by *paparazzi*, like Jimi at the Samarkand, or poor Kurt in his greenhouse, it was almost as if Munch couldn't allow himself to embrace his talent, couldn't completely escape those raging inner demons.

Consider the illustration of Munch's *Man and Woman* (*Mann og kvinne)* at the front of this book[21], the woodcut that provided the critical flash of inspiration for Alberto Bravin and Gregory Spawton. The man sits hunched over, his hands clasped around his head, as if in the grip of some hidden turmoil or shame. The woman next to him is unapologetically upright and naked. She appears both unreachable and sphinx-like, and it's the contrast between her inscrutable poise and her partner's collapse that gives the image its tension.[22]

The painting is often interpreted as a metaphor of the emotional distance between the sexes, the pain that comes when intimacy fractures, which reminds me of some raw and beautiful lines from the poet Philip Larkin:

Nothing shows why
At this unique distance from isolation
It becomes still more difficult to find
Words at once true and kind,
Or not untrue and not unkind.[23]

Some Munch scholars link *Man and Woman* to Munch's own turbulent relationship with his fiancée Tulla Larsen, especially his sense of love as something indivisible from anxiety and vulnerability. In this respect, the 'relief' inherent in his woodcut illustrations very much has a double meaning that is beautifully dramatised on *Woodcut*, the album. For Munch, the darkness was inseparable from the beauty, the *yin* and *yang*, that so appealed to Alberto Bravin and Gregory Spawton and inspired their tragic artist figure. As Munch himself once tried to articulate:

---

[21] Appropriately captioned *Let Us Begin Where It All Began.*

[22] Compare also the raw, uncompromising power of the woodcut version of *Mann og kvinne* with the ambiguous, swirling uncertainty of the oil painting that bears the same name.

[23] *Talking In Bed* by Philip Larkin.

> *"My sufferings are part of my self and my art... What is art really? The outcome of dissatisfaction with life, the point of impact for the creative force, the continual movement of life... In my art, I attempt to explain life and its meaning to myself. All art, literature, and music must be born in your heart's blood. Art is your heart's blood."*

Through Munch's startling originality, we can see just how complicated that process can be, epitomised in the quote that begins this book from the German printmaker, Ernst Ludwig Kirchner. A woodcut is not just an illustration; it's a window into the soul that may come at a great price to the one who opens it. That irresistible urge to explore both the self and the outside world has been inspiring artists across continents for more than a thousand years.

But what window does *Woodcut* the album open? The first thing that listeners will encounter is a glorious illustration based on a print by Dorset artist Robin Mackenzie, which Gregory Spawton views as an intrinsic part of the album, as well as a continuation of Big Big Train's tradition of striking cover artwork.

> *"I think one of the reasons why Alberto and I were struck by the word 'woodcut' in the beginning is because it's got a kind of heft to it. It has weight. It's physical. I think if we'd tried to create a woodcut print of a pastoral scene simply by drawing an image, or even experimenting with generative AI, it would have felt very wrong. It wouldn't have someone carving the wood, nor using this wonderful Victorian printing press to roll out the image itself. That authenticity matters both for the artwork and the music.*

> *"In the context of the culture that we live in today, I suppose you could say Big Big Train is a 'real' band. By which I mean we can play our instruments. We can perform whatever music we create in front of a live audience. That spontaneity and the freedom it offers will always be important for me. I think it's one of the most important things that distinguishes human creativity from that generated by Artificial Intelligence, since AI can only be retrospective and trained on what came before. We're very serious about the music we create, and I recall wanting to emphasise this to Robin because he shares a similar mindset about his art. He's a very creative individual, passionate and personable, so we hit it off right away."*

Reflecting on Spawton's thoughts about being able to take the show on the road, my mind turned to Yes's cycle of live albums covering their first tour with *Close To The Edge*, the *Progeny: Seven Shows From Seventy-Two* series. To be honest, at the time of their release, those albums felt like one of the aforementioned lavish box sets; a somewhat cynical exercise intended to beef up the coffers at the expense of affluent fans willing and able to buy anything in the name of completeness. However, I now view *Seven Shows From Seventy-Two* differently. When he talks about 'keeping it real' I think what Gregory Spawton refers to is the essence of live performance. It's the idea that you're hearing sounds absolutely unique to a moment that can never be expressed in exactly the same way again.

Furthermore, many of these great moments of performance are things that the artist had neither planned nor prepared for; they're created by a mind pushing outwards to connect with the world and suddenly finding a doorway where, before, there had only been a blank wall. If AI had been around in August 1969, would it have been able to redefine the US national anthem in the same coruscating manner that Jimi Hendrix did at Woodstock? Did Queen really know what kind of era-defining performance they were about to deliver at Live Aid? Like the rest of the world, whose collective jaw dropped instantly to the floor, would AI have seen it coming?

So now, when you listen to *Seven Shows From Seventy-Two,* although it's the same music, you appreciate more the fact that it's never the same performance. That Jon Anderson never sings the high note in *I Get Up, I Get Down* exactly as he did the night before. That Chris Squire's bass rhythms kept going their own way, night after night. As Gregory Spawton was so keen to emphasise, the wonderful thing about being an artist, or at least a human one, is that nobody knows which direction you might take next. Half the time, artists and musicians might not even know themselves. Which is why we still get goosebumps when we watch footage of Paul McCartney, Ringo Starr and George Harrison jamming on a Twickenham sound stage while they wait for John Lennon to show up, mucking around with chords, singing nonsense lyrics, until suddenly, without warning, you realise they've started to play *Get Back.*

It's this idea of spontaneity – of being creative, or not; of following your singular vision, or not; of finding a way to cope when your universe howls, or not – that drives the narrative of *Woodcut.* From beginning to end, we are locked inside the deepest hopes and fears of an artist trying to find fulfilment, reward and recognition almost in spite of his own human failings. It's not clear, nor really important, whether this individual is a tormented genius, like Munch, or just a talented individual with unfulfilled ambitions and a belief that one day they might achieve spectacular renown. Maybe, as Clare Lindley joked at the end of one of the interviews for this book, there's an element of autobiography in that interpretation – "It's all about the likes of us!"

The beautiful 1854 printing press used by Robin Mackenzie to create the cover illustration for *Woodcut*. The Albion Press was invented in the early 1820s by an Englishman, Richard Whitaker Cope, and its poetic name was likely chosen in response to the Columbian Press that had recently arrived from the United States. The Columbian Press, invented by the American George Clymer, was a similar metal hand press but the Albion became more popular because it was faster to operate and easier to repair.

R M
& COP
LON

The original woodcut block for the album cover alongside the ink roller. The inking process was featured in the *Inkwell Black*-accompanied *Coming Soon* trailer video, released in October 2025 prior to the official album announcement.

After the death of the Albion Press's inventor, Richard Cope, his company was taken over by John Hopkinson working under Cope's executors, Jonathan and Jeremiah Barrett. Hopkinson made a number of improvements to the mechanism, which was subsequently marketed as "Hopkinson's Improved Albion Press", with the names of Cope, Hopkinson and the Barretts imprinted on the header of the machine. After 1840, however, the style became simply "Hopkinson & Cope", which is the format used on Robin Mackenzie's Albion Press.

Close-up of the carved detail of Arcadia from the album cover for *Woodcut* created by Dorset illustrator and printmaker, Robin Mackenzie.

Big Big Train arriving at Sweetwater Terminus. All other services from this station are postponed until further notice.

Aladdin's Drum Cave, Sweetwater Studios

Aladdin's Mic Cave, Sweetwater Studios

This is a Rivera-modified, 22-Watt 2-Channel All-Tube Guitar Combo Amplifier with Tube Reverb and Tremolo. According to Sweetwater:

"Paul Rivera, Sr. started modifying guitar amps in 1968. After a stint at Fender in the early '80s, Paul launched his eponymous company in '86. Rivera's amp mods are the stuff of legend, and were in high demand by the who's who of Los Angeles session guitarists. Larry Carlton, Dean Parks, Jay Graydon, and Chet Atkins, Steve Lukather, Robben Ford, Rick Nielsen, Reggie Lucas, Tom Rotella, Tommy Tedesco, Vince Gill, Jerry Donahue, and Kerry Livgren of Kansas were among the wide variety of players who ultimately owned and used an original Rivera Stage 2 Mod. The customized Rivera circuitry made it possible for studio players to nail the perfect clean and lead tones all with one compact guitar amp."

For the recording of *Woodcut*, Rob Aubrey recalls:

"I think this was mainly used as a guide guitar amp when the band were all together in the playing room – we might also have used it for some of the violin solo parts. Once the drums and bass parts were put down we then went to different amplifier combinations and those parts were played in the control room, with Rikard using an array of models – Marshall, Sovtek and Plexi – and configs."

But the amp *did* have a key role on one song, *Dead Point* – as Rikard Sjöblom confirms:

"Because we kept quite a lot of the original track that I recorded while we were live in the room together I went back to the Rivera amp for that one."

21 April 2025, control room at Sweetwater Studios. Day 1 of recording *Woodcut*. Energy levels were high...!

Guitar corner, 22 April 2025. According to Rikard Sjöblom:

"I don't know why, but all the guitars just seemed to gravitate towards my corner of the room. Mostly, however, I just used my own three electrics: the Gibson ES-335, the white Fender Stratocaster [the RJS-monogrammed guitar familiar to many BBT fans] and the double-necked 12-string Harley Benton electric. Between the Fender (which is the white guitar in the left-hand rack) and the Gibson (on its own stand immediately to the right of the Fender) I think I used both equally, but in general I'd use the Fender mostly for clean and funky parts and also for some solos (the Counting Stars *solo for example), and the Gibson for crunchier parts and also most riffs. But I did play the Gibson for quite a few solo and melody parts as well. I also played one of the studio guitars – I think it was a Fender Telecaster – in the chorus of* The Artist. *That was tuned in what's called Nashville tuning, which is where you only use the octave strings of a 12-string set to get a light chimey sound."*

Pedal board setup for Rikard Sjoblom, 22 April 2025. Rikard explains his setup thus:

"The two fuzz pedals on the board are ones that I would have a hard time being without for certain songs with Big Big Train, with both of them being used in Apollo *for example. The Zvex Fuzz Factory [middle row, left-hand pedal] is a pedal that can make extreme self-oscillating fuzz tones and you can hear the effect in the first guitar solo of* Apollo*. It keeps the sustain for ages and doesn't gradually tone out – it just dies instantly! The green one [top row, first left] is called Swollen Pickle (a pedal Rob Aubrey often mentions because of the name – not the sound – as in "You do enjoy your swollen pickle, don't you, Rikard?"!) The reason I like it is because it delivers some really nice, thick fuzz tones and it's essential for some riff and solo parts. The footswitch, Push To Talk, is for speaking to Rob in the control room, and also the rest of the band while we were tracking (to save us from removing the headphones every time we needed to say something across the room!)."*

An array of legendary names in Oskar Holldorff's keyboard den, including Hammond B3, Mini Moog, Peak Novation, Yamaha YC61 and Wurlitzer. According to Oskar:

"The top keyboard on the right is a defective Hohner Clavinet that we sadly couldn't get a sound out of. The Clavinet rests atop a Fender Rhodes that we used extensively! It was an absolutely beautiful instrument in mint condition – the best Rhodes I've ever played. That said, it was only my second favourite instrument at Sweetwater, pushed into the runner-up spot by the Yamaha grand piano, which was just incredible to play."

Alberto Bravin trying out a new guitar in the Sweetwater showroom. No *Stairway*.

Nick D'Virgilio in the control room, late afternoon 24 April 2025. The main focus of the Sweetwater recording sessions was to lay down the drum and bass parts for the whole album.

Rikard Sjöblom recording electric 12-string guitar at Sweetwater Studios, 25 April 2025

Rob Aubrey and Rikard Sjöblom during evening guitar overdub sessions at Sweetwater Studios, 25 April 2025

The Hammond B3 and the MiniMoog ready and waiting. Fair to say that without these two legendary instruments, the history of prog (and just about every other genre of music barring Gregorian Chant) would not be the same. Both feature prominently on *Woodcut*, but my favourite moments are the blistering Hammond attack on *The Artist* and the heartbreaking Moog solo on *Light Without Heat* as The Artist finally accepts that Arcadia is a dangerous illusion. Writers often comment about the unique sound of the Hammond and the Moog, as if they produce music all by themselves, but as always, it's not what you've got, it's what you do with it that counts.

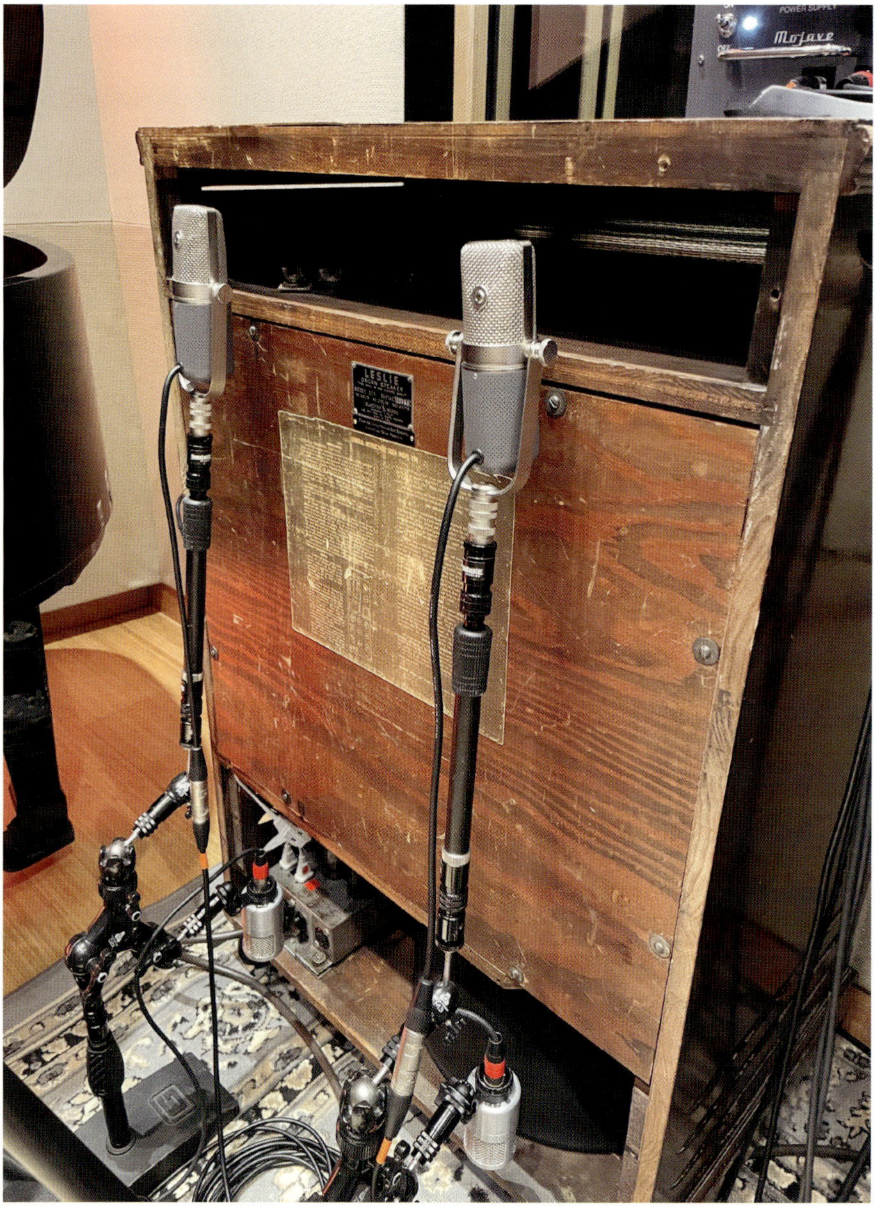

Mic setup for Sweetwater's beautiful vintage Leslie speaker paired with the Hammond B3 organ. This particular Leslie is a 21H model, which places its date of manufacture somewhere between 1951 and 1958. It's a beautiful working piece of musical history. One can only imagine the amazing sounds that have flowed through this stunning speaker down the decades.

Kittens in my mind I've always seen in black and white

Kit, check. Sticks, check. Cans, check. Drummer... waiting for NDV.

Nick D'Virgilio ready for
(yet) another take

Two progressive rock legends. Gregory Spawton with Rickenbacker bass at Sweetwater Studios, April 2025.

Alberto Bravin at the mixing desk at Sweetwater Studios, April 2025

That doesn't sound like the demo

NDV: *You want it in 23/8? Bring it on!*

Rikard: *Is it just coffee in that cup?*

You shall not pass. Gregory Spawton mans the barricades... his station in the main playing room at Sweetwater Studios.

Alberto Bravin tweaking guitar amp settings for Rikard Sjöblom at Sweetwater Studios, 25 April 2025

Amps, amps and more amps. It's not known how many of these go up to 11.

Sitting at the mixing desk for long hours can be tiring. Kneading out some shoulder tension in the control room, 25 April 2025.

Getting ready to unleash the mighty Taurus. Sharp-eyed musical readers might be able to name that tune from the strategically placed bass part notes on the iPhone.

Gregory Spawton unimpressed by Oskar Holldorff's best attempt at prog charades, 25 April 2025. Sacrificial farm animal decides to take a nap in Manhattan? Avian speaking parts encased in savoury jelly?

Rikard Sjöblom recording electric guitar overdubs with Oskar, NDV, Alberto and Rob Aubrey, Sweetwater Studios, 26 April 2025

Clare Lindley, Oskar Holldorff, Rikard Sjöblom and Alberto Bravin rehearsing, Sweetwater Studios, 26 April 2025

"Don't tell Clare!"
What happens in the studio,
stays in the studio.

I don't know when it started | This feeling I've a long way to go

Alberto Bravin at the helm of mission control at Sweetwater Studios

Oskar Holldorff in his keyboard enclave at Sweetwater Studios, 26 April 2025, about to record another section of *The Artist*

Rob Aubrey and Alberto Bravin overseeing a take in the control room at Sweetwater Studios, 29 April 2025

Studio notes from the recording sessions at Sweetwater Studios, 21 April 2025. Rob Aubrey explains:

"Studios and band setups can be complicated and every band has some unique requirements - probably no two prog bands have the same approach. But that's a good thing because we don't really want to use 'stock' or normal setups!

"Sweetwater is a wonderfully modern studio and gives you the ability to patch in different setups rather like an old style telephone exchange using a 'patchbay'. It allows any source (like a microphone, for example) to be plugged in anywhere in the studio, and routed through to the mixing console then into the recording computer.

"This sheet shows us what's happening - what source channel, what instrument, what microphone, where it comes from and where it goes to - so we can keep log of everything should a problem occur. In the studio, it may look like a mass of wires and interconnects but it's all very logical."

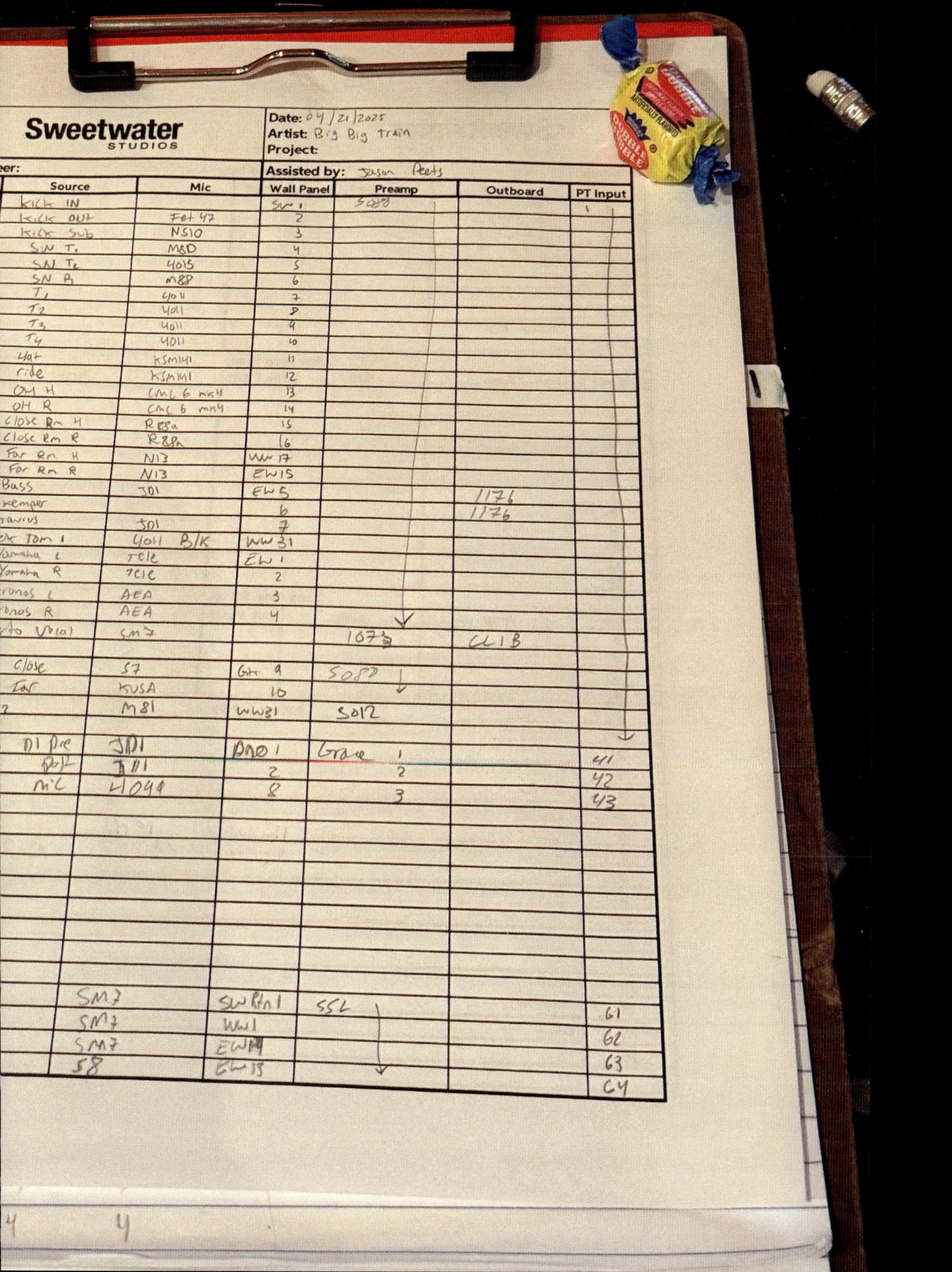

Sweetwater STUDIOS

Date: 04/21/2025
Artist: Big Big Train
Project:
...eer:
Assisted by: Jason Peets

Source	Mic	Wall Panel	Preamp	Outboard	PT Input
Kick IN		SW 1	5088		1
Kick Out	Fet 47	2			
Kick Sub	NS10	3			
SN T1	M80	4			
SN T2	4015	5			
SN B	M88	6			
T1	4011	7			
T2	4011	8			
T3	4011	9			
T4	4011	10			
Hat	KSM141	11			
ride	KSM141	12			
OH L	CMC 6 mk4	13			
OH R	CMC 6 mk4	14			
Close Rm L	R88a	15			
Close Rm R	R88a	16			
Far Rm L	N13	WW 17			
Far Rm R	N13	EW 15			
Bass	JDI	EW 5		1176	
Kemper		6		1176	
Taurus	JDI	7			
...k Tom 1	4011 B/K	WW 31			
Yamaha L	Tele	EW 1			
Yamaha R	Tele	2			
Kronos L	AEA	3			
Kronos R	AEA	4			
...to Vocal	SM7		1073	CL1B	
Close	57	Gtr 9	5088		
Far	KUSA	10			
...	M81	WW31	5012		
DI Pre	JDI	DAO 1	Grace 1		41
Post	JDI	2	2		42
Mic	4044	8	3		43
	SM7	SW Rtn 1	SSL		61
	SM7	WW1			62
	SM7	EW14			63
	58	EW13			
					64

With all of that background covered, I think it's time that we go deeper into this marvellous record. Listen to the brief but beautiful opener, *Inkwell Black*, with the album in your hands. Does the cover seem to be drawing you into a secret and mysterious world? Like Eustace before the Dawn Treader, the swirling form has a bewitching, almost hypnotic power, brought to life by a stately adagio of violin, cello and clarinet. Imagine walking down the winding trail into the heart of the forest, trees closing around you as the roar and clamour of the urban world fades into a hush. Now go further, loose twigs snapping under your feet, leaf fall transformed into a carpet, footsteps sinking into the loam to hide all trace of your passing. Ahead, you sense rather than hear the indistinct silver-belled murmur of a stream where the mossy smell of nature seems irresistible: green, earthy and potent like never before. The bright afternoon dissolves into a twilight realm where time is suspended. You are here and nowhere. This is the magical world of *Woodcut*.

> *"We felt it was important to have real strings right at the top because they're wooden instruments and they immediately immerse you in a particular kind of mood. And, of course, Maddie Wegg's clarinet has that lovely, mossy, sylvan tone that also evokes thoughts of greenwood and forests,"* says Clare Lindley. *"My partner, cellist Brian Mullan, and I did additional work on* Inkwell Black *to give it more of an authentic string quartet feel. The parts were essentially there, but sometimes you need to adapt the arrangement when you want to incorporate real stringed instruments rather than just using synths. It can sound a little unreal, for example, if you don't have four parts playing all the way through, or when you have too many instrument sounds because the piece was played using ten fingers on a keyboard."*

And there were other ways in which the band retained the authenticity of the physical instruments, as trumpet player Paul Mitchell (Maddie Wegg's partner) remembers.

> *"There was a section on* Arcadia *where Alberto had written the part, and the bottom note was slightly lower than the alto flute would physically reach. I think we also tried using the clarinet, and during the recording process, we had a lengthy conversation about whether we should use a sample to produce the low note. But in the end, we decided to stay within the limits of what the instrument is capable of producing, and that's what Maddie plays on the record."*

Inkwell Black provides further insight into the precision and ingenuity with which Alberto Bravin assembled all the various contributions from his bandmates during the initial gathering of material for *Woodcut*. It's a melody that you'll hear again, and when you do, it will be completely different to your first encounter, as Gregory Spawton explains.

> *"One of the liberating things about working on a concept album is that even just a small idea or a fragment of a song can assume an importance in the overall flow that's as important as a fully developed song. In a way, the only downside is that sometimes you have the fragment and it serves its purpose in the musical or vocal narrative, and you're thinking, 'Oh, but I don't want to let go of that just yet.'*
>
> *"So, more often than not, we would try to build those moments out, and there are a few little connecting pieces where Alberto took the original motif and made it more substantial. And that has the effect of drawing the threads together and making the album feel more cohesive. That's exactly what happened with* Inkwell Black. *It's a slightly odd chord sequence. We liked it, but it took us a while to figure out how to bring it back in a different part of the album. I think listeners might be surprised when they hear it next."*

If the purpose of *Inkwell Black* is to ground our imagination in the mood space suggested by the cover illustration, it certainly succeeds. Perhaps another reason why the artwork exerts such a powerful hold is due to Robin Mackenzie's method of seeking inspiration in nature, as the illustrator explains.

"I actually find it very hard to create a piece if I haven't been to that location and immersed myself in it. A lot of my personal work is based on the coastline, so I often go up to the Hebrides and Shetland to experience those wild places. For me, that physical connection is an innate part of the process because you're trying to cut the feeling of the wind in your face, and the rain dripping from the leaves and branches. You can't capture that by looking at a photograph in a book because it's not sensorial.

"And, it's not just a question of topographical detail. It's about drawing upon something deeper, such as the atmosphere of a location and your memory of how it felt to be alive, in that place, in that moment. So, I'm not trying to capture everything when I draw; it's more about the essence. That's what you bring back in your carving. And I can only do it if I can take myself back there. If I know what it was like."

Coincidentally, it's similar to how Gregory Spawton sought inspiration when grappling with writing the lyrics for the song *The Lie Of The Land*.

"My home is very close to the River Stour, and between our house and the waterway, there's a dense thicket of woodland adjacent to some fields. Even though it's quite a small wood, and still close to a large town, it's wild nature that's been left to its own devices. It hasn't been tamed or refined in any shape or form. And so I had to really battle through brambles and thorns to make any headway, which is where the line 'No place for a man' *comes from. And then, almost as* The Lie Of The Land *says, I stumbled into a glade that the sunlight had lit up, and there was this remarkable feeling of stillness and peace. So, I tried to channel that feeling into the song and the moment where The Artist finds the piece of heartwood and everything all clicks into place."*

Following *Inkwell Black*, the second track, *The Artist*, plays a crucial role in setting the scene and introducing the character whose experiences drive the story. On any other album, it would rightly be considered a classic Big Big Train epic; here it's simply the introduction. According to Alberto Bravin, the track actually *was* an epic, a 15-minute piece composed by Rikard Sjöblom, from which Bravin cleaved the opening to form the basis of *The Artist*, and then used a second section of the original song right at the end in album closer *Last Stand*. He almost sounds a little guilty at the memory.

> *"There was one piece of Rikard's that I couldn't really find a way to include. So, I took the beginning and end but set aside this long middle section. And Rikard was naturally, 'Hey, what happened to my song? I really liked that piece of music!'"*

If the guitarist was irked, he generously gives no hint of it as he recalls the reimagining of his creation.

> *"I'd found this Rickenbacker guitar in a local store, and I was mostly just playing around with it for the first couple of days, trying to figure out what kind of sounds I could make with it. That's when the opening riff came to me, which almost had a kind of Flamenco vibe to it. And then I began building it up by adding bass, keyboards, and drums – creating drum parts with the keyboard. It segued into this really big piece with a long instrumental section in the middle, very fast and quite Genesis-like.*
>
> *"The voicings and the harmonics are pretty out there, even though it's just standard tuning on the guitar. But I think it has a lot of energy, and the section we used really helps to launch the album. And that's what matters, not whether this section or that section gets used. The instrumental part might always come back again in a future project."*

While recognising the inevitable tension that can arise within a band comprised of multi-talented musicians and songwriters, Spawton shares Sjöblom's opinion and feels that *Woodcut* is a testament to Big Big Train's collective sense of purpose.

"It happened to all of us. I know NDV had some parts of his songs altered, and there were various things of mine where I thought, 'I don't remember it that way.' But that's how we worked on Woodcut. *All the songs have to serve the story, so we couldn't be too sensitive about our own individual pieces. It's part of being in a band. Sometimes you just have to take a step back and think, 'This isn't about me, or my ego, it's about the album and the band as a whole.' Having Alberto as the designer-in-chief helped because we just had to trust him with the songs and the music and say, 'Over to you to make this work.'"*

Oskar Holldorff agrees.

"If everyone did just what they wanted, I don't think the album would have been anywhere near as good. It might have been interesting, but I think there needs to be a certain level of control. So yes, while it sucks sometimes to spend a lot of time working on an idea that is voted down, it's part and parcel of life in a seven-piece band. The upside to having someone mastermind a record like Alberto did for Woodcut *far outweighs the drawbacks of having some creative limitations imposed. On balance, I think it's a much better way to organise if the personalities in the group will accept it."*

One thing that stands out when speaking with members of Big Big Train is their team spirit and genuine sense of togetherness. Sometimes, when bands are interviewed, there's a feeling that the collectiveness on display is more for the benefit of the cameras or the audience. And sometimes, of course, there's no pretence at togetherness at all, which is when creative and personal differences burst into the light, as journalist Tim Coffey describes:

"Throughout rock history, countless bands have had to undergo major changes or break up entirely because everyone couldn't get on the same page. From losing their creative direction to making some of the most questionable decisions in rock history, some of the

greatest rock bands of all time have come to terms with the fact that their internal chemistry had started to wane."[24]

Although Big Big Train has had its own fair share of personnel changes through the years, some more intense than others, for the most part, the parties involved have remained on amicable terms. And two studio albums into what may be termed 'the Bravin era', founder member Gregory Spawton feels that the present line-up is building momentum once again.

"I'm proud of every version of Big Big Train that there's ever been – from the earliest albums with Ian Cooper, Andy Poole, Martin Read and Steve Hughes, through the period with Sean Filkins and then the very important years with David Longdon. But while I cherish all the band's music, today we're a band that is working at a different level. I think this is the very best work we could do at this point in our careers, and it's as strong as anything we did in the past."

I think this is very evident, both in how the band interacts with one another and in how they individually talk about their colleagues. In this regard, the beautiful vocal arrangements that Big Big Train can produce feel like a case of art imitating life. Oskar Holldorff has an interesting theory about this.

"I feel like vocals can sometimes be a bit of an indicator of the mood within a band. If you're able to harmonise together and appreciate your place as an individual within the whole, I think it's a powerful symbol of teamwork. Every voice is important, both on its own and collectively, and it's hard to fake that feeling. It requires a lot of trust because you're very exposed when you're singing with someone unaccompanied. If one person wavers, the whole group wavers. And if you think about it, humans have used choral singing to come together for centuries. When you harmonise, you're creating

---

[24] 'The 10 biggest conflicts within rock bands' by Tim Coffey, *Far Out* magazine, July 2023.

> *something and tapping into an emotion that instinctively pulls you together. I think we all feel that's an important part of our music, both professionally and personally."*

When it comes to prog pastoralism, Genesis's *A Trick Of The Tail* always looms large, and there are certainly fronds of that masterpiece curling around parts of the trunk in *The Artist*. But as The Artist's struggles intensify, and the pace of the music accelerates, elements of another great prog standard may spring to mind, specifically *Freefall*, the opening track of Camel's 1974 album, *Mirage*. And this feels like a very apt comparison because the character we first encounter in *Woodcut* is in an emotional freefall he seems powerless to control.

Lyrically, however, *The Artist* is a different kind of prog beast to its celebrated predecessors. The song introduces the album's core theme: the pressure of creativity and the loneliness that comes with possessing a singular vision only you can bring to life. As W.B. Yeats observed, to follow it – or not – may be a painful, almost existential, choice:

> *The intellect of man is forced to choose*
> *perfection of the life, or of the work,*[25]

This is the dilemma that makes *Woodcut* both a classic narrative concept album and also a 'psychological' record, very much rooted in the 21st-century schizoid society in which we find ourselves. In a world of uncertainty, where objective truth feels increasingly elusive, and our ability to express authentic emotion through art is being muddled by technology, a woodcut feels like the ultimate riposte to AI and the indiscriminate slop of large language models. If, as Munch wrote more than a century ago, art is the heart's blood, then it must matter that music, poetry, painting and sculpture are created from heartbeats rather than hard disks; that the price of every word, note or knife stroke has been one less second on earth. Artists are in a constant battle against the deadline of their own mortality, to set everything down while they

---

[25] *The Choice* by W.B. Yeats, 1933.

still can, a struggle which may not be good for one's mental health, as the writer Laurie Penny observed.

> *"If you want to make a great painting, you're going to have to stand in front of a piece of canvas scratching away with oils for hundreds of hours. If you want to write a decent novel, you're going to have to shut yourself away with your pens and your keyboard, talking largely to people you made up in your head. That sort of thing isn't normal. That's what Byron meant, I'm convinced, when he wrote that 'we of the craft are all crazy'."*[26]

Perhaps this is how the meme of the 'tormented artist' originated. Painters, authors and songwriters often struggle with their inner demons to create their works, and, in the moment of creation, the art form takes a piece of their being as the price for its imprisonment. Maybe there is a double edge to the lines:

> *Who'd have thought creation*
> *Would take so much away?*

Because once they make the final brush or knife stroke, stop the tape or type 'The End', no artist is the same again. And the audience may never be the same either. How often do we hear fans say 'Your music changed my life and gave me hope'? Or courage, or confidence. That's a human, not an artificial, connection, a meeting place where we still find the best of what we are, and one that Big Big Train has always invited us into with deep sincerity.

It also speaks to one of the paradoxes of art: artists themselves can never feel the emotion they inspire in the audience encountering the work for the first time. This is the idea expressed in Emily Dickinson's *I Would Not Paint A Picture* that it may be better to be the receiver than the giver:

---

[26] *Requiem For A Scream*, Laurie Penny, September 2017.

And wonder how the fingers feel
Whose rare – celestial – stir –
Evokes so sweet a torment –
Such sumptuous – Despair.

There's one other crucial aspect to all of this, and it can be summed up in a single word: risk. With AI, there is no risk. Type your prompt. Spew out an image. Vary it. Vary the variations. Vary them some more. Trash them all. Start again. Nothing to lose. This is the very antithesis of creating a woodcut, as Robin Mackenzie describes.

"Woodcut illustration is very raw. You can't hide with it, you can't overdo it, you can't repaint it, and you can't add anything over. So, once you've committed, it's there physically. Stone carvers have a lovely way of saying that the image or the sculpture is already in that piece of stone. And it's similar for me. I love the idea that you're almost working in reverse, taking away what's not there and allowing the light to appear from the darkness."

Few will argue that through his wonderful design for the album's cover, Mackenzie was able to capture something innate and profound that enhances listeners' appreciation of the music. But he is not the only artist to allow light to emerge from the darkness. Another *Woodcut* visual collaboration was so striking that even the members of Big Big Train themselves began to think differently about who the troubled and tormented figure at the heart of their story might be.

"It made sense to introduce the album with The Artist *as the first single,"* explains Gregory Spawton. *"Firstly, because he's the main protagonist and we felt it was a very direct way to bring people into the world of* Woodcut. *From the outset, it gave audiences someone to root for, someone with whom they could empathise and engage. In that sense, the visuals needed to do more than simply set the scene; they had to create an element of intrigue and mystery. We wanted audiences to question how The Artist arrived at this point in his life, and, more importantly, what might happen to him next.*

"But this created a bit of a dilemma. Even in a world dominated by streaming platforms, singles typically need a promotional video, and The Artist *is not your typical 4-minute radio edit. There was a lot of discussion about how we could dramatise this complex figure and the transformation he undergoes."*

The filmmaker tasked with that creative challenge was well accustomed to transforming extended musical ideas into beautiful visual fantasies. Miles Skarin, from video and VFX production company Crystal Spotlight, had previously worked with Big Big Train on the video for *Miramare* from *The Likes Of Us*, as well as collaborating with a multitude of other prog artists. When it came to positioning *The Artist* as the entrance to a much bigger conceptual world, Skarin was comfortable with the extended and layered nature of the story, having contributed whole album visuals for Steven Wilson's *The Overview* and a full-length feature called *Ocean Sounds* for prog duo, iamthemorning.

The contrast between the ancient woodcut methods employed by Robin Mackenzie and the digital video technology used by Skarin is fascinating. Both artists have brought their talent and skill to bear using *Woodcut* as the common inspiration. But whereas one employs techniques that have been passed down through centuries of craft and endeavour, the other wields tools and processes that are cutting-edge in a different way, and can sometimes seem as if they're developing in real time.

"It's wonderful how these distinctive visual art forms, whose origins are millennia apart, have combined to make the world of The Artist more tangible," says Gregory Spawton. *"Because we had previously worked with Miles on* Miramare, *we already had a good appreciation for his work. Of course, it's a nice bonus that he has worked with other prog musicians and genuinely likes the music, but he is a gifted filmmaker and storyteller, and he quickly grasped the essence of The Artist's dilemma. His animation is fantastically contemporary in terms of his production techniques – that's evident from the video*

– and yet his development of The Artist – the way the character looks, the way he moves, the attention to detail in the creation of his home studio – has this marvellous fairy-tale feel that's reminiscent of traditional hand-carved puppetry. It's exactly the right atmosphere for the narrative, and it beautifully complements the look and feel of the album artwork established by Robin [Mackenzie].”

“During my initial call with the band, we talked about what The Artist should look like,” recalls Miles Skarin. *“It's interesting that there's no description of his appearance in any of the lyrics. Clare had a sense of him being older, worn down by his troubles, perhaps a little unkempt, as if he was losing touch with everyday life and no longer caring about making an effort. That gave me a starting point.*

“I was also conscious of the fact that we would need to bring the character forward into other videos and filmed pieces. So, I spent a lot of time thinking about the animation design, not just his superficial appearance, but also how he would move and perform in different environments. The idea of using a wood grain texture for his appearance originated from an earlier concept in which the character's form was composed of multiple slices of wood, creating an illusion of solidity as the camera moved around them. But I think character works really well as we've represented him.”

In contrast to the irreversible nature of Robin Mackenzie's wood carving process, Skarin's challenge seems almost the exact opposite: how do you commit yourself to a creative path when your choices are virtually unlimited and can be undone by a keystoke? Even a superficial glance at the software used by modern digital filmmakers reveals a dizzying array of sliders and settings that almost defy you to choose a starting point. I was struck, however, by the similarity between Robin Mackenzie's description of 'trusting the process' and how Skarin explained his own methods.

> *"For me, that freedom is one of the things that's most rewarding. Often, animators strive to be as efficient as possible, animating only what is required for a specific shot to minimise the amount of detail they need to create. However, I prefer to build the entire environment and fully populate the scene, as this gives me more control and freedom to experiment. And although there are almost no limits on the objects you can create and how you can manipulate them, in reality, there are certain fixed steps that you follow when creating an environment or a character: processes like building the 3D model or defining the range of motion you want them to have. So gradually, step by step, you create the thing you're working on, and as it takes shape, new possibilities emerge, so your awareness of what it might be, or what it could become, is constantly changing and adapting also."*

Skarin's work has certainly changed even the band's awareness of who their creation might be. For Clare Lindley, author of the lyrics for the track *The Artist*, the transformation of the character in the video was revelatory.

> *"It was a real moment seeing this person, who'd existed in my mind for such a long time, brought to life by Miles. Although I had a sense of what The Artist looked like, the lyrics were always focused on his thoughts and feelings rather than his appearance. He was more of a presence than someone whose face I could have described to you in great detail. It's a wonderful feeling, therefore, to see something, or rather* someone, *that you've created and become very attached to in your mind's eye, become real. When I watched the film, it was almost like seeing him for the first time. It's as if he's been set free to live a life of his own outside of my imagination."*

In contrast to the certainty and confidence of the real-life creatives who have worked to create the visual world of *Woodcut*, the opening lines of the song *The Artist* convey with brilliant psychological detail the loneliness and dread of an artistic life where the light is hard to come by. A life that is literally being lived upon a knife-edge.

Searching for perfection
But second-guessing everything

How heart-breaking must it be:

To carve a thousand birds
And never hear them sing

While still never being able to shake off the dread of inadequacy, that your life's work, ergo your life, has no value to anyone else?

Never enough
Dreams slowly burned and turned into ash
Go through the motions
Keep showing up
Carve to feel nothing
Work for the silence
Cut for relief

Contrast this anguish with Robin Mackenzie's description of how he first began to develop the illustration for the album cover.

> *"My focus was on sketching very fluid and quite indistinct shapes, with lots of circular brushstrokes that owed more to the feeling and atmosphere of the place than any particular detail. Quite often, pieces will start for me as a movement of the brush. The movement informs what it is I'm drawing, and gradually, from those loose and very free brushstrokes, you start to find your way into the illustration. But it's not a pre-conceived thing. It's almost like there's something there that you need to find."*

This casting outwards into the shapeless void of the imagination can be a daunting task for any artist, regardless of their talent or experience.

And for human, as opposed to computer generated, creativity, it's an obligatory and pioneering act of exploration that encourages others to follow them. As such, it's one of the things that makes the artist uniquely valuable (some might say irreplaceable) in society.

> *"Certainly for artists of all stripes, the unknown, the idea or the form or the tale that has not yet arrived, is what must be found. It is the job of artists to open doors and invite in prophecies, the unknown, the unfamiliar; it's where their work comes from, although its arrival signals the beginning of the long-disciplined process of making it their own. Scientists, too, as J. Robert Oppenheimer once remarked, 'live always at the "edge of mystery" – the boundary of the unknown.' But they transform the unknown into the known, haul it in like fishermen; artists get you out into that dark sea."*[27]

That last sentence seems redolent with prog rock possibility, but imagine the anguish when you simply can't find that 'thing' you're seeking? When you can sense its presence but never truly capture the form because the wild, dark sea threatens to drag you under. I think The Artist's blade is sharpest, therefore, not just because of the keenness of the edge but also because of what it's cutting into. When people reach their limits, both body and soul may become mediums for their hurt, as Richey Edwards of the Manic Street Preachers once notoriously demonstrated by carving '4 Real' into his arm when questioned by a sceptical journalist. There's a sense of that rage in *The Artist* with its discordant, Ottoman-inflected guitar and fiddle, and a crazed Hammond solo against which D'Virgilio's hammering kick drum patterns resemble someone pounding their temples out of sheer frustration.

It seems clear that we're in new territory for Big Big Train, possibly because there is a new lyrical voice in the band. Most of the songs that speak to the 'internal' (*The Artist, The Sharpest Blade, Albion Press, Dead Point*) were written by Clare Lindley, whereas those that deal with the

[27] *A Field Guide to Getting Lost* by Rebecca Solnit, 2005.

'external', such as when describing landscapes or veering towards the universal and the philosophical, generally come from Gregory Spawton (*Arcadia, Counting Stars, Last Stand*).

Initially, *Woodcut* was recorded as a collection of musical 'scenes', instrumental pieces with a clear narrative purpose but no actual lyrics, as Alberto Bravin explains.

> *"To begin with, there was just the music. We understood the story and what might be happening in different scenes, but there were no lyrics as such. From that, I recorded a version with a complete set of guide vocals, where I strung together words or phrases to try to express some kind of feeling. And I think that helped Clare and Gregory because then they had a 'mood board' for where the emotion might land once the lyrics were set to music. Even if I'm just singing 'La-la-la', or about the sky, or whatever, I still try to put my heart into giving a performance. Afterwards, there were still a few other developments. Once I have the proper lyrics and can really understand what the writers are trying to say, I might need to adapt how I sing the lines. Maybe I need to make something softer, or adjust the rhythm to accommodate extra words. These are all subtle details that emerge as the songs come together."*

The lyric-writing team of Spawton and Lindley then faced a relatively imposing task to deliver the actual lines for their bandmate to sing.

> *"I think at the end, Clare and I were talking at least a couple of times a week, not just about the wider story, but divvying up who would take ownership for writing each particular section,"* says Gregory Spawton. *"It was almost like we were writing instalments for a series, and we'd be asking for drafts because one of us would need to know the plot to carry on writing the next episode. So, there was a very strong sense of continuity and collaboration even though we were both working flat out in our own 'lyrics cave'."*

> *"I thought it was going to be difficult to write the lyrics with so much of the instrumentation in place,"* says Clare Lindley, reflecting on the fact that most of the narrative detail came after the music. *"I was quite daunted by that because I've tried it before and it's proven to be quite a challenge. However, this album was 'easy' to write in the sense that we had the plot worked out, so we always knew what a song or even a verse might need to say to move the story along."*

In conversation, it's clear that both Lindley and Spawton are thrilled by their new collaboration and how their respective writing styles have blended as they fully dramatised the high concept first envisaged by the bass player and Bravin in Oslo.

> *"In terms of writing the lyrics, Alberto and I had a feeling that Clare would be able to do a great job with the storytelling,"* says Gregory Spawton. *"Because you can tell by the way she communicates day-to-day that she's a natural wordsmith. And for my part, although the kind of writing that I gravitate towards is part of the band's DNA – the rural scenes and subjects that involve history or landscapes – there's a lot of stuff on* Woodcut *that isn't in my comfort zone, which Clare handles with aplomb. Having her – and NDV on one of the songs* [Warp And Weft] *– take up the lyrical reins relieved the pressure on my shoulders. Again, you have to remember that writing a concept album is a lot trickier in many ways than writing a collection of individual songs. The famous example is* The Lamb Lies Down On Broadway, *which everyone knows was Peter Gabriel's grand design. But right at the end, even Peter was running out of steam for filling in the details and needed some support from Mike Rutherford and Tony Banks. So, for me, it was perfect to have Clare write a collection of lyrics that were a more natural fit for her writing style than they would have been for mine."*

> *"For some months, possibly even a year before I actually sat down and started writing* The Artist, *I was gathering words and images*

that supported this concept of a tortured artist," explains Clare Lindley. *"I carried a notebook around because I was always a little bit worried that if I didn't write something down when it came to me, I might forget about it later! I actually wrote the verses for* The Artist *in the studio at Sweetwater as it was being recorded by the band. If I remember correctly, I think Oskar was doing some of his piano parts for what became* The Lie Of The Land, *and I thought, 'Well, I'm doing nothing in the studio today, and I've got all these notes, so let's start trying to put this together.'*

"It's a bit funny that I was sitting there thinking, 'Okay, so how am I going to open this album, then?' and, almost right there, that sentiment became the opening lyric, 'I don't know how it started'. It's almost like my own private in-joke. But all of those opening verses just fell into place within the space of half an hour, and I remember turning to Greg and just saying, ever so casually, 'I've just written The Artist,*' and thinking to myself that this songwriting business was quite easy. And he just looked at me and went 'Uh-huh', because he knows that it's not! And it came back and bit me later on when I had to do more work to beef up the choruses. I must have literally toiled for hours, moving things around, trying not to repeat ideas I'd subsequently written elsewhere. Getting those lines just right was incredibly difficult in the end. So, Greg is right. Songwriting is a messy business!"*

You sense an element of friendly rivalry between the pair as they worked to complete the body of lyrics required for the album.

"*Yes,*" says Spawton, glancing at Clare Lindley, who is staring at him with a playful grin, almost daring him to dig a hole for himself. "*While it certainly wasn't anything intense or personal, there was a degree of friendly competition involved in the sense that I'd get a set of lyrics from Clare and I'd be thinking, 'Oh my God, this is fantastic, I'd better not let the side down here!' I think we both felt a responsibility to each other, as well as to the rest of the*

> *band, to reflect back as much quality as possible in the ideas we were exchanging. And from that, a real feeling of trust has emerged. It's fostered a very strong lyric-writing partnership that bodes well for the future."*

Sometimes with concept albums, the high-level idea can become a little unsteady once you delve into the details of the story. At other times, there's a temptation to pad things out with flashy instrumentals because there's a double (or triple) album to fill. One of Big Big Train's achievements with *Woodcut* is that the band manages to avoid both of these pitfalls. The story developed by Lindley and Spawton is dramatic and thought-provoking, while the musical arrangements masterminded by Alberto Bravin never flag or feel disconnected from the lyrics. And like the music, the words have space, yet manage to avoid sounding overly crafted or verbose. This economy of expression makes the emotional impact of the story all the more credible, never more so than in the majestic central section that forms the bulk of *Woodcut*.

In *The Lie Of The Land*, The Artist ventures (as characters often do in Gregory Spawton songs) to find solace in nature. There are reminders of the lush arrangements of *I Talk To The Wind* by King Crimson, with its glorious flute solo that brings to life a bird joyfully singing in the woods. Here, the calming effect is created by a heartwarming melody of piano and mellotrons, and a sense of liberation takes hold.

> *The lie of the land*
> *Carries me onward*

While solo piano has always caught the attention in Big Big Train classics, most famously on Danny Manners' signature introduction to *East Coast Racer*, it's noticeable throughout the album how Oskar Holldorff's expressive piano is used to clarify and give texture, whether – as here – alongside Bravin's mellotrons (all the mellotron sounds on the album are more or less straight lifts from the original demos), rippling underneath the vocals in the manner of Tony Banks on

Arcadia, or taking centre stage on *Counting Stars*. But as Alberto Bravin is quick to point out, Holldorff's versatility across a range of instruments really shines out on *Woodcut* in a way that perhaps hadn't been so obvious on *The Likes Of Us*.

> *"Oskar plays most of the keyboards on the album – grand piano, Fender Rhodes, Hammond B3, even Wurlitzer – and then I play the mellotrons, most of the Moog pieces and Rikard plays the organ on his songs. But my favourite Oskar moments are when he's just going all out on the Hammond. I don't think we expected that. Rikard is normally the master of the crazy keyboards, but Oskar just unleashed this raging, wild, distorted Hammond solo, which was really cool to hear live in the studio."*

> *"Rikard was very generous in letting me play some of those sections,"* says Holldorff modestly. *"He grew up with the Hammond, so it's a big part of his musical identity. But on* Woodcut, *he mostly focused on guitar, so it made sense for me to contribute, looking ahead to when we'll have to perform these songs live. To be honest, those sessions were the first time that I'd been able to record using a real Hammond organ, and it was a little daunting, because with the drawbars and the expression pedal, you have so many options to shape the sound. Plus, of course, there's no sustain, so you have to adjust your technique because the only way to extend the note is literally to hold down the keys. It's a bit of a rocket ship to pilot. Ultimately, I just tried to follow my instincts as to what the song might need, and it was great fun to let rip and see what would happen!"*

Just as in the third section of Spawton's earlier epic *Beneath The Masts*, or in the panoramic violin solo in *Hedgerow*, there is a glorious sense of elevation. The Artist's mind seems to be soaring above his weary body through the separation of the physical and the emotional, and the band responds by picking up the pace, which becomes exultant and eager. It's as if The Artist senses some great discovery is close at hand and is impatient to rush ahead. And what he finds is ecstasy.

It's all I was searching for
This heartwood is here for me
Though hard and so heavy
The way back home is clear
Sure as an arrow's flight
A burden now made light

There's a paradox here. The heartwood is heavy yet also a burden made light. Perhaps it's wise to be wary in case things are as ambiguous as they seem. Be careful for what you wish for. Your dreams might just come true. Gregory Spawton agrees.

> *"I chose the title carefully because the 'lie of the land' is a geographical term, but also a hint that perhaps things aren't quite as good as they seem. 'Lie' means false or not to be trusted in that context. I think it's wrapped up in the concept of darkness and light that runs through the album, this idea that things have both a positive and a negative identity. And that becomes more important in later songs as events unfold."*

A notable feature of *The Lie Of The Land* is Alberto Bravin's phenomenal ability to span a very broad emotional range, from the relatively downcast opening to the song's exultant ending. The way he powers through the climax and conveys the excitement as The Artist discovers his inspiration is one of the album's key moments.

The opening of *The Sharpest Blade*, with its insistent fiddle and folky Celtic rhythms (echoing the fervour of Big Big Train's earlier *Folklore*), took me back to my teenage years when I first listened to Kate Bush's sumptuous *Ninth Wave* suite, in particular the song *Jig Of Life*. Clare's first studio lead vocal with Big Big Train creates a sensuous, mystical atmosphere. All distractions fade into the background as The Artist begins carving in a trance-like state, where individual dust motes become identifiable in the sunlight, nature's heartbeat coalescing with his own. Because of this lush aura, another association that came to mind was with the cave of the Lamia, where Rael placed his trust in beauty blind. And here, it feels as if The Artist is doing the same thing.

> "The Sharpest Blade *began in one of those quiet moments when, in a different time or place, I might have just been flicking through my phone,*" recalls Lindley. "*But I was in a teaching room in between giving music lessons, and I just began strumming some different chords on guitar, trying to find a chord progression that I liked and then adding a melody line for the verse. The fiddle introduction was actually more of an afterthought, something I just noodled over the top before I sent it to the others, but I've become quite attached to that little part. It seems to fit the mood really well. It's a bit spooky. A bit dark. There's a presence there.*"

But is this vision too easy? The knife has its own compulsion, and The Artist has no choice but to follow, as if he's been possessed. And there are some phantasmagorical elements lurking in the background. Voices that come in the night, hints of buried emotional trauma. The violin's single note is relentless, tugging, nagging; it won't let The Artist settle until he pushes himself to collapse and beyond. And what is this force? Why is it so eager? Isn't that in itself a warning, a subtle allegory of living in a society where it sometimes feels as if forces beyond our control are moving us into an unclear future in spite of our better judgment?

Again, I can't help but think of the sterility and inhuman nature of art created by generative AI, particularly because these images that appear so perfect on the surface are often marred by abnormalities upon closer examination. Most telling of all, AI has no intuition. And it's surely one of the most human of all fragilities to perceive the danger but carry on regardless.

In terms of the narrative, Gregory Spawton agrees that the song is an important part of the sequence.

> *"It's the right song, in the right place, at the right time. What I like about* The Sharpest Blade, *and this is true of any good song for me, is that you can sit down and play it acoustically, just with guitar and vocal, and it sounds great. But you can also turn it into something that the entire band can get their teeth into, and make it a showcase for what we do together. And that's kind of how it's mixed on the record. You have Clare singing her lead as a solo at the beginning, which feels very intimate, and then gradually the rest of us come in around her. And when Alberto adds his vocals to the chorus, and you have their two voices together, that's quite a spine-tingling moment for me. Rikard and NDV made some contributions, but* The Sharpest Blade *is primarily Clare's song, and she did a brilliant job with it."*

The song title *Albion Press* was actually inspired by the beautiful 1854 printing press used by Robin Mackenzie to create the cover illustration for *Woodcut*. Remarkably, Mackenzie discovered his Albion machine rusting in a shed where it had lain untouched for almost 50 years. The idea of bridging the centuries through an ingenious device like a mechanical printing press has obvious connections to earlier Big Big Train songs that celebrate Victorian innovation. Originally, the song was to have been entitled *First Press*; however, the idea of Albion also stirs something folk-like and mythical, evoking a sense of place that is everywhere yet nowhere, which fits perfectly with the mood of *Woodcut*.

Albion Press is one of the album's foundational pieces. It begins with an absolute Sabbath of a riff from Rikard Sjöblom, one that's guaranteed to crush it in any close-packed, tight-walled concert space where people shake their rock god hair (or the rock god hair they once had). This segues into a relentless Rickenbacker bass groove around which are wrapped lithe slivers of electric guitar that could have come straight from Prince's *I Could Never Take The Place Of Your Man*.

And yes, you read that correctly. For this is where Big Big Train gets deep down and dirty as the devilish spirits that were lurking in the background suddenly cut loose and shake their stuff. Spawton's playing is so funky you can practically see the bass vibrations, while Sjöblom's quicksilver phrases flicker like flames in turbulent air, accompanied by some luminous playing by Oskar Holldorff on the Fender Rhodes piano. The groove is like the soundtrack for a dance of the dead – an experimental contemporary dance troupe would surely have a ball – and you can imagine a cavalcade of contorted shapes, our animal spirits come to life, performing a fervent dance of glee as The Artist moves towards the press.

> *"The bass riff on* Albion Press *started as something that bears no resemblance to what you hear on the album,"* says Spawton with a smile. *"It was actually just a little theme that I hummed on my phone. To be honest, I wasn't even thinking of it as a bass part. On the video I sent to Alberto, I might have suggested it could be played on a bell, and later on, I think it does get picked out on the glockenspiel. But he transformed my little tune into this heavy, distorted bass riff, and it was a pretty big surprise to have this monster groove come into my life. And, of course, NDV loves that kind of thing too, so we had a great time getting it down in the studio. I think* Albion Press *has some of my favourite moments of Nick and me playing because the concept gave us the freedom to be a little more uninhibited, whereas on a conventional song-based album, we might have felt more constrained."*

Oskar Holldorff agrees that the concept album format gave the band more freedom to explore possibilities.

> *"I usually like to arrive very rehearsed before I go into the studio, so I know exactly what I'm going to play and can make the best use of the time. However, that was more difficult on this occasion because we arrived at Sweetwater straight from touring in the US and Canada. Although* Woodcut *had been progressing in the background, our immediate focus had been on the tour set list and ensuring we were prepared to play the old songs.*

"I think Rikard and I, in particular, were looking at ways we could find different sounds and approaches to express the original themes that were in Alberto's demos. I tried to leave a bit more room for improvisation in the studio, knowing that when we got to Sweetwater, I would have all these tools and instruments at my disposal. I guess I was giving myself a little bit of a challenge in that respect. I prepared the pieces that I thought might be the most challenging to work out, but mostly it was just a matter of assembling them in the studio together. There was one moment on Albion Press *where Rikard and I riffed this little* 'OK Computer' *motif over the chorus. And it just came from sitting at the Rhodes with no direction in mind, and thinking, 'What kind of pattern lends itself to this particular sound? How might it relate to the story at this point?' If I'd been recording at home, or if I'd prepared something in advance, that probably wouldn't have happened."*

And what happens next is what might have followed if Luke had taken Vader's hand and surrendered to the dark side. Trust your feelings. It's better than it's ever felt. Sure enough, the majestic melody that swells as Alberto Bravin sings:

Pictures in my mind I've always seen in black and white
I never thought the colours could change
Right before my eyes

is a tidal wave of pure emotion, and one that quite overwhelmed me on first listen. It's a high point for the band, too.

"Alberto has some wonderful moments throughout Woodcut," says Spawton. *"When you're recording lead vocals, you obviously need to ensure the performance is in tune and in time. However, if you're not moving the listener through the combination of words, melodies and chords, it can sound a bit sterile. But what Alberto, like David before him, does so well is squeeze every drop of feeling out of each note. There are moments in the studio when you're either playing*

together or just watching and listening to him perform, when you think to yourself, 'Wow. Capture that take. That's the one.'"

Another subtle but significant presence in the mix here is Paul Mitchell on trumpets. Although Big Big Train is justifiably celebrated for the colliery brass sound that gave so much emotional heft to many of the band's earlier releases and live performances, these resources were often used more sparingly across entire studio albums than the 'legend' of the BBT brass ensemble might lead you to think[28]. With *Woodcut*, however, it's noticeable that Mitchell is credited on nearly every track, reflecting a different approach to deploying brass instrumentation compared to what may have been the case before.

"I think the songs on the album each have their own style or mood, which determined my approach in terms of the brass instruments," says Paul Mitchell, sitting in his home studio with neighbour-friendly, sound-absorbing panels on the walls behind him. *"On some tracks, the trumpet has more of an 'orchestral' role. My part sits underneath the arrangement and I'm playing along with a melody that adds texture, colour and depth. In other places, however, it's much more up front: the sound is brighter and it's more distinctive in the mix. Actually, many of the trumpet parts on* Woodcut *are multi-tracked sections, so I'll have to work out how to recreate that on stage using harmony effects and octave pedals."*

There's an echo there of Clare Lindley's observation about the difference between stringed instruments and string samples?

"Yes, it's the same principle for brass instruments. With a keyboard sample, you can easily add another brass instrument simply by holding down a key. But with a real instrument, it's far more personal and organic. Even with the best sample, it's only a recording

28 The first Big Big Train album to feature the brass ensemble was *The Underfall Yard* and brass arrangements were used on almost every subsequent album (with the notable exception of *Grimspound*, although brass parts were developed for the live version of *A Mead Hall In Winter*) up to and including *The Likes Of Us*.

of a single note, not the individual way each trumpet player crafts their sound. Because we each have a unique appearance, our facial muscles give our playing a signature of its own. Plus, of course, we have to breathe! So, while it's easy to flick a switch to select the voice and press five keys to create an ensemble effect on a keyboard, it won't sound anything like five separate musicians playing together.

"In fact, we did try layering me playing five different parts on some sections before deciding it was too much," reveals Mitchell. *"On a few tracks, I tried using the flugelhorn, but I didn't like how that sounded, so I reverted back to trumpet. However, we found other creative ways to develop the sound. As an example, there are passages where we doubled the line with a synth patch rather than using an additional brass track. That gives the music a very different colour, so it might not register at first how the segment has been arranged. A piccolo trumpet with a synth on top sounds completely different to a standard B Flat trumpet, but it's still essentially a trumpet part.*

"You can also create atmosphere by using different microphones. For instance, using a ribbon mic gives the trumpet a much darker tone and reduces some of the instrument's natural brightness. Rob Aubrey also positioned several ambient mics around me while I was playing to produce a wider soundscape. With a single mic, the notes would sound as if they were coming directly at you, when, in reality, a trumpet sounds very different if you're adjacent to it rather than being right in front. All these small details helped make the brass arrangements more interesting and provided Alberto and Rob with more options to work with."

We're used to hearing the trumpet as a ceremonial instrument, and I believe it's a testament to the level of detail in the production that when you listen carefully to the lavish climax of *Albion Press*, you can hear Mitchell's rising trumpet fanfare anchoring the surge, subconsciously triggering that joyful and stirring emotional response we associate with uplifting ceremonial music. And at other times, as on *Chimaera*, you can discern the texture of the multi-tracked trumpet playing a long melody line underneath the rest of the arrangement.

Returning to the Oslo origins of the album, the emotional crescendo of *Albion Press* also brought to mind Munch's epic canvas *The Sun*, which would have been hanging in a nearby gallery on the day Bravin and Spawton made their fateful visit to the Munchmuseet. Dazzling and munificent though it is, Munch's star is profoundly inhuman. I sense something similar here: the duality of the infernal presence hidden within the euphoria of a glorious yet unruly burst of life-affirming creativity. Just as when Macbeth was granted visions by the witches and reeled in confusion:

> *This supernatural soliciting cannot be ill, cannot be good...*
> *And nothing is but what is not.*[29]

The moment seems to beg the question of whether anything that drives The Artist to such extremes can be trusted to be worthy of the sacrifice. Maybe this is why artists are tortured, because they are the ones who dare to try and find out. The fact that *Woodcut* is pushing us to address these kinds of questions is a testament to the power of its concept.

Either way, this euphoric and triumphant joy is the emotional high point of the record. Nothing will ever be quite like this again.

> *"I believe that you've created a metaphorical universe in which you can express your darkest fears. In one aspect, yes, I believe in ghosts, but we create them. We haunt ourselves, and sometimes we do such a good job, we lose track of reality."*[30]

---

[29] *Macbeth*, Act 1 Scene 3, by William Shakespeare.

[30] Laurie Halse Anderson in *Wintergirls*.

It's probably worth reflecting a little on the suggestive and paranormal elements that start to make their presence felt in *Albion Press*, since these are an important part of the world of *Woodcut*, as Clare Lindley explains.

> *"For a time, when we thought the supernatural presence might become more of a defined character, I did some research into malevolent wood spirits. Often, these sprites and shades are portrayed as being quite bucolic and benevolent, but I was looking for something darker. And I found an Eastern European character called Leshy, who is vindictive and spiteful towards humanity, not because he's evil* per se, *but because he dislikes people entering his woodlands with their axes and fires. His mischief is a form of revenge on our thoughtless intrusions. He'd rather not have to frighten us because he'd prefer it if we just weren't there, but since we are, he's going to serve us up some terror. And I liked the juxtaposition of something ancient and rooted in folklore with a very modern concern, such as the impact humans are having on the natural environment."*

Throughout the band's career, Big Big Train songs have often drawn on traditional stories and folklore elements, either directly in the lyrics and music or indirectly through their atmosphere. Primarily, these have been rooted in English traditions, such as the pagan character of the Green Man, dramatised on the cover of the band's *Wassail* EP and in the mask worn by singer David Longdon on stage. But nearly every culture has tales and myths that link urban society with something much wilder and more primitive; a rich tapestry of folklore unfurled across centuries that serves as either a benchmark for progress or a reminder of how much of our connection with the earth has been lost.

From the early Middle Ages until quite recently, for many people living in the rural countryside of Britain and other parts of Europe, the wild otherness of nature was something that could seem untamed and threatening. Ancient superstitions about the dangers lurking in the woods and waters were not immediately swept away by modern inventions, such as the motor car, telephones or electricity. The fear of the unknown influenced people's folk beliefs, even in relatively well-educated and worldly communities. Sometimes, spiritual explanations were the most effective way to explain unexpected events and outcomes that would otherwise cause trauma and psychological suffering.

One of the main differences between modern society and that of our ancestors is our attitude towards time. In earlier centuries, time was both influenced by and measured through close observation of the seasons, rather than by human-made devices such as watches and clocks. Much about the visible world was beyond our understanding; therefore, assigning key aspects of its routines to deities and mythical figures was the most logical approach. In his *Dictionary of Greek and Roman Biography and Mythology*, William Smith writes that:

> *"The early Greeks saw in all the phenomena of ordinary nature some manifestation of the deity; springs, rivers, grottoes, trees, and mountains, all seemed to them fraught with life; and all were only the visible embodiments of so many divine agents."*

Accordingly, it was an everyday fact that spirits, like Leshy, jealously guarded their territory and might punish careless humans who trespassed upon their domain. But on the other hand, spirits and deities could also be helpful if treated with respect, allowing a person to be blessed or rewarded by befriending certain spirits or behaving in a particular way to court favour. And throughout Europe, different cultures created their own versions of the cryptic forestal[31]: the Huldra and Skogsrå of Scandinavia, the Waldgeister of Germany, the Dames Blanches of French Lorraine and the Aos Sí of Celtic mythology.

---

[31] Apparently, there is no official English word for *forestal*. But readers of Stephen Donaldson's *The Chronicles of Thomas Covenant* will be familiar with the term, which is used to describe the ancient guardians of the forests in Donaldson's Middle-earth equivalent, The Land. In that spirit, I hope a little creative wandering beyond the confines of the Oxford English Dictionary will be forgiven. If you haven't read the novels, but have a thing for epic fantasy sagas (this is prog, after all), you might enjoy them!

These divine figures symbolised the sacredness of nature, acting as guides for the virtuous, and delivering retribution upon those who came with intent to harm the trees. They were important to fertility rituals, acted as patrons of hunters and shepherds, who were believed to have a closer bond with the realm of nature, and had a key (and now modern-seeming) role in reminding human society of its integral connection to the wider ecological world. In this respect, some might interpret the events of *Woodcut* as a trial for The Artist, punishing him for the transgression of removing the heartwood from its natural setting.

In *Woodcut*, of course, the forest is the most prominent natural setting, and it features throughout the album in several different ways. At the beginning, the cover of the trees is portrayed as a place of tranquillity and relaxation, but it soon becomes the scene of fevered agitation as The Artist finds his heartwood and rushes back to his studio. Later, the forest is described as a lavish Arcadia of almost preternatural beauty before transforming again, this time into a sinister and malevolent setting where our darkest fears are personified.

These dichotomies highlight an important aspect of the forest in our culture, in that it can represent both physical and psychological characteristics. In ancient times, fierce predators such as wolves, bears and wild boars roamed the woods and forests of Europe, and their menace was further amplified by an array of mystical spirits believed to be even more dangerous, as they were said to exist beyond the physical world. In folklore, therefore, the forest was frequently depicted as a place where individuals experienced spiritual transformation, confronting inner demons or achieving a higher understanding of themselves.

In his book *The Uses of Enchantment: The Meaning And Importance of Fairy Tales*, Bruno Bettelheim articulated this idea, which seems to perfectly sum up the drama of *Woodcut*.

> *"Since ancient times, the near-impenetrable forest in which we get lost has symbolised the dark, hidden, near-impenetrable world of our unconscious. If we have lost the framework which gave structure to our past life and must now find our way to become ourselves, and have entered this wilderness with an as yet undeveloped personality, when we succeed in finding our way out, we shall emerge with a much more highly developed humanity."*

Or, if that seems a little too highfalutin, you might prefer this sassy epigram by author Icy Sedgwick instead.

> *"On one hand, the forest can provide bountiful resources, and on the other, it contains things that can and will kill you."*[32]

If you go down to the woods today, perhaps you had better go in disguise after all. As we shall see, the psychodrama of the forest plays a significant part in the story of *Woodcut.*

If *Albion Press* opens a gateway to a world whose deeper designs are as yet unclear, on the surface, *Arcadia* is a place that every Big Big Train fan will want to visit. After the intoxicating highs of the night before, the song begins tentatively and tenderly as The Artist confronts his creation in a state of sleepy bewilderment. But as in Ernst Ludwig Kirchner's monumental woodcut, *Junkernboden*[33], a dazzling panorama of nature is laid before him – a true "window into the soul" as Kirchner himself proclaimed in the quote that opens this book.

What was once a monochrome flatland has been transformed into a landscape of almost unimaginable beauty and colour. It's the encapsulation of all the rural idylls we have known in Big Big Train's music:

[32] *The Folklore of Forest Protectors and Guardians*, Icy Sedgwick, February 2024.

[33] Landscapes and the restorative powers associated with nature were fundamental artistic and philosophical concepts for Kirchner, especially during his early career.

a perfect vision of heath and hedgerows, meadowlands, rivers and streams, where butterflies may be curated and all of nature thrives. Gregory Spawton is well aware of the connotations.

> *"Alberto has a particularly strong view of the importance of the songs I've written about the land or landscapes, because, for the last 15 years, that's been a core component of the band's DNA. And, while I obviously don't disagree, I was conscious in tackling* Arcadia *that this is a subject that comes fairly easily to me, and I've already written a lot of words of a similar type. So, I didn't want to end up narrating something on autopilot. I spent a considerable amount of time thinking about what* Arcadia *meant in the context of the story and* Woodcut *as a whole. Where is The Artist in his life at the moment he encounters this world? What is important to this particular scene and song? I felt this was the best way to write something that would still sound familiarly Big Big Train while also having something fresh and notable to say."*

Listeners will also be struck by Alberto Bravin's control of pace on *Arcadia* as The Artist explores the scene. It takes exquisite musical judgement to begin delicately, then build to a soaring crescendo that gives enough space for the rest of the band to reach a triumphant finale around him.

But sadly for The Artist, it's a fleeting vision. Too soon, he finds himself cast out of paradise, which poses another thought-provoking question: would we prefer not to have an experience or emotion if the realisation that we'll never feel that way again might crush us? Can humans ever bear too much reality?

I say this because there is some wonderful, hidden gravity at work here. Former Big Big Train singer David Longdon's sensibility seems to run deep in places, as evident in the closing lines of *Arcadia,* with their strong echoes of Longdon's bravura performance on *Voyager.* Close your eyes and you can easily imagine him singing:

And inside a storm is raging
High against the world
Steadfast and determined
I will find a way
Will make my way back home

In spite of myself, I feel a longing to hear that. Not because I think David would have sung *Arcadia* more immaculately than Alberto – I don't believe anyone could – but simply because I'm human. I miss the man and his music. Regret is what humans do. As we so often witness in Big Big Train music and the band's recent history, nostalgia and 'what might have been' are both a blessing and a burden, which brings us back to the paradox of light and darkness that *Woodcut* is built upon. It's the rhythm of balance and change that you shouldn't try to alter or bend to your will, and I believe this is the point of Arcadia in art and literature. Because ultimately, at some point in our lives, we all want the things we can't have. And if we were to get them, it might very well drive us mad.

This soon becomes apparent in the dizzying vocal labyrinths of *Warp And Weft*. This track closes out the second side of the album and marks a dramatic shift in mood.

> "*When NDV submitted this song, I think we felt it slotted right into place in the storyline,*" reveals Gregory Spawton. "*It has this disturbed, unsettling energy that perfectly describes The Artist's manic phase as he strives to return to Arcadia. I think there's a bit of a Gentle Giant influence with the complicated time signatures and the layered vocal parts. Those were written and arranged by NDV, and then the rest of the band recorded their individual parts separately. The singing is very complicated, but we have six vocalists, including new member Paul Mitchell, who can each hold down a vocal part, so we have the potential to do some very sophisticated harmonies and arrangements.*"

> *"The seed of the song goes way back,"* says Nick D'Virgilio. *"The opening guitar riff had been with me since I was about 16! I'd play it endlessly, revisit it from time to time, but never knew quite what to do with it. It just floated there, unfinished, waiting for a home. Somehow, this album provided the right spark. All of a sudden, that old riff made sense. Within a couple of days, I had the vocal lines, the melodies – everything fell into place."*

Previously, there was a strong sense of an external force guiding The Artist over the finishing line, but now it's as if the powers-that-be have become hostile. The diabolical presence that was hinted at in *The Sharpest Blade* is manifesting itself:

> *Something stirs beneath the grain*

And that something is horrific.

Accordingly, D'Virgilio's lead vocal is manic and ferocious, capturing all the drama of The Artist's battle with these demons, and completely different in character from the sunshine personality we normally see behind the drums or hear in other vocal performances, such as *The Florentine* and live renditions of *Telling The Bees.*

If the definition of insanity is repeating the same task over and over with the expectation of a different result, then The Artist is clearly losing his mind. The song seethes with an almost uncontrollable energy; it's like an obsessive-compulsive disorder set to music, and along with its bristling Led Zeppelin chord stabs, as well as Nick D'Virgilio's brilliant and constantly shifting time signatures, the dense, counterpoint vocals create the impression of an unstable mind fragmenting into multiple personalities as The Artist searches frantically for the elusive spark that will return him to Arcadia.

For Spawton, it was one of the most intense and enjoyable sessions of the entire recording process.

> *"I think* Woodcut *might just be NDV's best drumming ever, but I particularly remember the 'play out' to* Warp And Weft *in the studio. Nick was on fire, and I almost wished we could have gone*

on forever. Of course, you have to bring it to an end at some point, but it will be a hugely enjoyable track to play live. It's a weird dichotomy because, in that moment, we were having an absolute blast recording the music, whereas in our story, it's a point of real crisis for The Artist."

Now all these different identities are clamouring in a blur of pain and confusion as the otherness makes its presence felt.

I see it move – I feel it breathe
The more I cut – the more I see
It's changing shape, it's changing me

With regard to Gregory Spawton's earlier comment about playing live, it's clear that the band are looking forward to performing *Woodcut* before audiences, even if the complexity and continuity of the album will present a few challenges.

"As we're recording these albums in the studio, we're more aware now that we need to be ready to perform them live," confirms Spawton. "And in fact, when we were developing Woodcut, *we did have conversations where we'd ask each other, 'Okay, how will this sound on stage?' That wasn't always the case when Big Big Train was more focused on studio work because we might combine a drum part from five different takes and never have the drummer play one version straight through. While that's interesting from a production perspective, for the musician, it can be tricky during rehearsals because they're thinking, 'I don't actually remember playing this!'"*

Nick D'Virgilio echoes these sentiments as he recalls the difference between Big Big Train's earlier studio methods and the approach required for live performance.

> *"Back in the day, I didn't edit my own drum tracks, so what you hear on those early recordings is a composite of multiple individual performances. When we revisited* East Coast Racer *years later for* Ingenious Devices, *I re-recorded the drums because, over time, performing the song live had given me the chance to refine it and shape the drum part into something tighter and more intentional. It wasn't a complete overhaul, but I did simplify certain passages and play different fills to give the piece more cohesion.*
>
> *"With* Woodcut *and more recent Big Big Train albums, the process is a lot more deliberate. I work out the drum part in advance, we rehearse it thoroughly, and in the studio, we fine-tune the details until everything feels locked-in. And that's what we record as a complete piece of music. That attention to detail makes a huge difference to how consistent the drum sound is, both in terms of technique and feeling, and I hope fans will be able to appreciate it on this recording."*

Big Big Train fans might know that a similar composite process was used for the renowned cornet solo that closes out *Victorian Brickwork*. Originally recorded by Ben Godfrey, the album version was a masterpiece of editing wizardry by Andy Poole, who painstakingly constructed a complete solo from numerous different takes. Even though the piece has been performed live many times since, the studio version diverged in style and phrasing from how a trumpet or cornet player might have played the solo if it had been recorded in a single take. For *Woodcut*, however, Paul Mitchell played all of the brass parts more or less as a whole, which should make the transition to the stage simpler.

> *"Although we might have dropped in the odd correction here and there, almost all the trumpet sections were recorded as complete pieces of music. For me, that was more rewarding than just playing them four bars at a time. Recording longer phrases and sections gave me more opportunity to shape the music, which goes back to the individuality in trumpet playing that I mentioned earlier.*

"My old trumpet teacher used to say that the trumpet in your head has to be as loud as the one in your hand. What he meant was that you always need to have the sound you want to make firmly in your mind before you attempt to produce it on the instrument; otherwise, it simply won't come out as you intend. When you can record these longer pieces of music, I find you can get more into the flow and emotion of the music because you're better able to combine those two instruments: the trumpet in your mind and the one you're actually hearing.

"It was great to have more creative responsibility, even though it required a bit of a marathon session at Aubitt Studios, where I was recording for almost two full days. By the end, I had started to switch to the piccolo trumpet to give myself a bit of a breather. When you begin to feel fatigued on the trumpet, you tend to play a little sharp, so switching to the smaller instrument helps overcome that. You use such specific facial muscles when playing the trumpet that even with a short break – just a couple of weeks off – you really notice the difference. When it comes to performing some of these longer sections on tour, I will definitely need to be match fit!"

Something has to give, and *Chimaera* begins with a brighter, more optimistic arrangement, almost as if a considerable amount of time has passed during which The Artist has been able to relearn his craft without the creative jet fuel of the supernatural. And it feels like a patient, steadfast process, one measured in the 'warp and weft' of each day, gradually leading him deep into his visionary world. The simple kick drum strikes a repetitive beat: a methodical, almost plodding tempo to suggest it's been a steady, almost hair-shirted pilgrimage, allowing The Artist time to reflect on his own mortality, on the need to face the future and carry on. But to his surprise and unease, he starts noticing the work of other hands in the Arcadia he thought was all his own. These sentiments are conveyed in an impassioned and soulful vocal from Oskar Holldorff, one of several instances throughout the record where other band members assume lead vocal duties.

> *"I wasn't actually supposed to sing that part,"* reveals Holldorff. *"Originally, Greg had sung it on the demo, and it was a real spine-tingling moment, one of my favourite bits of the album. So, when he offered it to me, I was surprised but also really determined to give it my all. It's naturally in my register, which made it easier. Beyond that, I think you can sometimes produce your best work when you're not expecting to do something. You don't have any time to overthink things. And it's a really lovely piece of music to perform."*

I'm sure many listeners will agree that the contrast between Bravin's and Holldorff's contributions on *Chimaera* is beautifully judged, and that Oskar's introduction is a genuine 'wait for it' moment.

In prog, when thoughts turn to home, as in *Supper's Ready* or *Ritual*, it's normally the final stretch, the glorious resolution. But on *Woodcut*, the very notion is a source of utter bewilderment. Where is home? And, as another tortured artist once asked: is this the real life, is this just fantasy? If the latter, whose fantasy? Has The Artist gone so deep into his fractured psyche that he is seeing visions created by multiple versions of himself, like in some *Black Mirror*-esque dystopia? Or have other artists, poets and thinkers been lured here, seduced by their personal demons then left to wander, leaving traces of their unraveling in their wake. Prometheus himself, before defying the gods to steal fire and earn everlasting torment, was also a creator, a craftsman. Once more, we're left to contemplate the personal cost involved in pursuing an artistic vision to its end.

> "Chimaera *is a pivotal moment,"* observes Gregory Spawton. *"In many ways, everything seems bright and optimistic, and The Artist has managed to regain the world that he's created. But gradually, he begins to detect that all is not as it seems; that there*

> *might actually be something here that could be harmful and damaging. So, on the one hand, you still have the beauty of Arcadia shining through, but there are these little warning signs, like one of those horror movies where everyone is smiling rigidly all the time, even when pretty dark things start happening. So the lines are meant to be blurred and the tone of the music is deliberately offset from what is really going on in the story."*

Almost inevitably, therefore, we reach the *Dead Point*, a liminal space where all dimensions and possibilities are perfectly balanced. This is pure supernatural gothic, the *Blair Witch* moment of the album – a place where even nature seems afraid, and one can imagine a sickly scent of decay roiling the senses. Beyond the glade, The Artist sees that the trail leads deeper into the forest, and we sense that to continue down this path is to pass the point of no return. But to make this choice, he will need to pass a perilous figure in the clearing, whose vaguely human form belies the fact that he has "the universe in his eyes".

> *"We were really conscious of the need for the music to track the story in terms of intensity and emotion,"* reveals Oskar Holldorff. *"Clare, Alby and I lived at NDV's house during our time at Sweetwater, and we had a lot of late-night discussions about where the story was going. And one of those conversations actually led us to completely rework* Dead Point *because the original demo version didn't seem to fit with where we were in The Artist's journey."*

> *"It's where we meet the 'monster' in our story,"* says Spawton. *"And it is a perilous moment. But I think The Artist is attracted because the danger brings a heightened sensation of being alive, and that's an emotion we can all relate to. I think it's that* yin *and* yang *tension again. A little bit of risk can be a positive force that helps us move forward in life. But sometimes – and it seems that very creative people are particularly susceptible to this – you can overreach by taking unnecessary risks, or by becoming addicted to something that gives you that temporary high. So, in the end, The*

Artist is faced with a choice: becoming lost to this imaginary world he has created, or stepping back to try to accept real life as it is."

The song's title was carefully chosen and has an interesting autobiographical context.

> *"The title* Dead Point *is a term I brought across from my other passion apart from music, which is climbing,"* says Clare Lindley. *"When you're reaching for a hold on a rock face that's just beyond your reach, you might need to jump to make the connection and momentarily lose all contact with the wall. It's called a dyno. And it requires power and total commitment. And ideally, you want to grab your target hold just when your body's momentum pauses and before gravity pulls you down again.*
>
> *"But in that instant, you're effectively weightless – your body has zero velocity – so it's like you've created a 'dead point', which is the stillness or liminal space between these two opposing forces. And that's effectively what's happening in the story. The Artist's fate feels like it's in the balance. He's arrived in this sinister, in-between place, but we're not quite sure where he is, or if the character in the glade is real or imagined. That's why I thought of it as a 'dead point' where different possibilities are waiting to be revealed. And now The Artist will have to summon all his resolve and fully commit himself if he's to make contact with reality again."*

The clearing is where the pure and idyllic atmosphere of *Inkwell Black* has been transformed into something precarious, as Lindley explains further:

> *"At this point, I feel the character is in a place where he is vulnerable like never before. It was something that was there in the earlier songs where you had the sense these dark forces were exploiting The Artist's creativity, but now he's wide open and defenceless. And I hope the story has brought people to the point where they can believe that this is the kind of thing that would happen. Like Gregory said,*

it's the same as an addiction. Craving your heart's desire even though you know it's destroying you. It's difficult for anyone to stop when the allure is the most exciting stimulation they've ever felt or experienced. In this case, The Artist has to surrender the one thing that seems to give his life true purpose. And in the next track, Light Without Heat, *I think the extent of his heartbreak becomes clear."*

The corruption of Arcadia was the inspiration for the collaborative reworking of *Dead Point*. Once they had decided that the original idea wasn't appropriate for the storyline, Oskar Holldorff explains how the band came together to create a new piece of music during the recording sessions at Sweetwater Studios.

"We held back a little bit at first because we were conscious of not using precious studio time to improvise an entire song. However, I think the risk of leaving the track as it was, and disrupting the album's flow, was greater than the potential cost of spending a session to rewire it. What's interesting is that at this point, there were no lyrics for the song. I think it shows the strength of the concept as a whole that we could convey it musically even though Clare hadn't yet put the story into words."

"Dead Point *uses the melody of* Inkwell Black, *which up to that point had been a bit of an orphan on the record,"* says Gregory Spawton. *"It was a fragment written by Alberto and me, and it opens the album, but we hadn't really found a way to bring it back. There was a considerable amount of head-scratching around a piano that afternoon, but after four or five hours of work, we had a completely new piece that everyone had written together. And that's not something we could have done remotely. You'd need 5,000 emails to iron out everything and another 5,000 emails to swap different demos. Being able to do it on the fly was a golden opportunity, and it was one of the best days at Sweetwater, with everyone firing on all cylinders, reacting to each other's ideas, and creating an entire piece of music almost in real time. It's a real ebb and flow piece of*

> *music because that's literally how it was written. A true team effort in every way."*

Rikard Sjöblom agrees.

> *"That song was one of the first I heard from Alby, but he wasn't really happy with it and was still making changes right up until we arrived at the studio. One afternoon, we just gathered together around the piano with everyone throwing out ideas – 'Try this... how about that?' Really spontaneous stuff. Later, we went to our stations and played live, trying to create something from those ideas. That's how the song gradually emerged. The heavier guitar riff that cuts in halfway through was an idea I had while we were jamming, and then everyone embellished it together. So, when you listen to* Dead Point, *you're hearing a wholly original piece that didn't exist until we created it that afternoon at Sweetwater Studios."*

The occult presence confirms to The Artist that he needs to get out of here (wherever "here" may be). There can be no more doubt that whatever he thought he'd created was not entirely of his own making. But such is the nature of addiction that even in this moment of critical danger, when surrender would surely mean oblivion, The Artist is still deeply attracted:

> *This close to danger is when I feel most alive*
> *How can this be wrong?*
> *Why can't this go on and on?*

The question is almost childish in its refusal to admit reality. Why can't this go on? Because it will kill you, that's why. This bipolar struggle is expressed in a defiant, almost confrontational Moog solo from Bravin, supported by some crunching guitar patterns and D'Virgilio's insistent hi-hats, with their echoes of Alan White's precise rhythms in the first part of Yes's *Awaken*. The ghostly echo '*And on... and on...and on*' feels like The Artist's obsessive personality being severed and dissolving forlornly into the æther. A choice has been made. But this is not the end of the story. If the complexities of *Dead Point* resolve in a very satisfying finale, *Woodcut* still has plenty of twists and turns to reveal.

Although The Artist has realised he must try to return to reality, this proves more difficult than it sounds. The movement begins with *Light Without Heat*, a beautiful ballad about disappointment and shattered illusions. The melody reprises the joy once felt in *The Lie Of The Land*, an echo picked out in delicate 12-string guitar, with a respectful nod along the way to the mood and style of Wishbone Ash's classic *Time Was*. But now it sounds like the promises of ghosts. Bravin's plaintive delivery is a lullaby to broken dreams until the moment halfway through the song, where he unleashes an astonishingly raw and heartfelt cry of anguish that seems to come from nowhere. It's a spine-tingling piece of vocal control and precision.

It seemed to be another time
It seemed to be another life
But it seems to be a lie

This is followed by a wonderfully emotive solo on the Moog and the first of a quartet of great guitar performances in the final movement by Rikard Sjöblom, an extravagant yet disciplined performance that is particularly notable for its intensity of feeling.

> *"Rikard's musicality is incredible,"* says Spawton admiringly. *"I mean, technically, he's insanely gifted. He can play slow, fast, this tempo, that tempo, whatever you like. But there's not a moment in the day when he's not thinking about music in some shape or form. It's like complete immersion for him. So, when you're in the studio and you give him a guitar or a keyboard, he has the ability to literally pull an idea out of nowhere. If you say, 'This is the situation, play something that feels right,' he'll do it on the spot. But if you say, 'Not quite what I had in mind,' he'll instantly adapt it, or play something completely different, or vary the sound. It's like he has this endless fountain of creativity that's always producing ideas,*

and I think, even amongst musicians, Rikard's intuitive ability to realise any idea right off-the-cuff is a special gift.

"By contrast, I've always been more of a pre-planned kind of guy in that I like to sit down on my own and figure out my parts and structure all the chord sequences. So for me, it's more of a process and a methodical kind of thing, whereas Rikard just grabs lightning from the bottle. I think Rikard's playing on this album is some of the finest work he's ever done. He makes a massive contribution to telling the story through the music, like on a track like Light Without Heat, *but there are still plenty of 'Rikard moments' where he cuts loose and goes crazy. It's one of the things I love about being in a band, in that all of our musical personalities are pulling together, but there's still plenty of individualism in the mix."*

Alberto Bravin agrees and shares Spawton's admiration for their colleague.

"Sometimes in the studio, the bigger challenge is figuring out how to channel all of Rikard's creativity into the framework of what a song, or the album, needs. That's particularly true on a concept piece where so much of the music is interrelated. There was one moment on Arcadia *where I was engineering and he played something on the second or third take, and I said, 'That one. That's the solo.' And Rikard went 'Maybe I could just change it a little bit here...' And I said, 'No, leave it. That's the solo. That's the one. It's perfect. Let's move on!'"*

"I went into this album being more focused on mainly being the lead guitarist," says Rikard Sjöblom modestly. *"Because perhaps I've kind of been a jack of all trades in the past, jumping around doing guitar parts here, keyboard parts there. This time, aside from a little bit of Hammond organ, it's really just electric guitar for me on* Woodcut. *All the acoustic guitar pieces were recorded by Greg, Nick, Clare or Alberto, while Oskar and Alberto covered keyboard*

duties. So, it was nice for me just to be focused on giving 100% to the lead guitar role, which I didn't have to do before when the two Daves[34] *were present, and trying to bring my style of playing to the fore. I didn't really approach any particular song thinking, 'Oh, this is a big moment for me now.' It was really more a matter of going with what the song needs."*

That reminded me of the words of another great guitarist, Nuno Bettencourt, when he said in conversation with Rick Beato in May 2023:

"The importance of soloing in a song really defines a guitar player for me. You have a choice. You're either going to be going for the Guitar Olympics and show off technique or speed purely for the sake of it. Or you're going to let this amazing song you love guide you, talk to you, and show you where to go... and what you hear equals what you feel, meaning you're being reminded that there's a physicality and an emotionality to all of this. A fire, and a want, and a passion to an instrument."[35]

Once again, we're back to human choices and the powerful emotions that underpin art for both artist and audience. As I listen to the final movement of *Woodcut*, I doubt whether Sjöblom has ever made better choices on a Big Big Train album.

As an example of how the whole is greater than the sum of its parts, *Dreams In Black And White* is the kind of track that the internet may revere in years to come. I envisage YouTube music documentaries about 'Prog In The Twenties', where a white-haired yet still spritely Alberto Bravin sits behind a mixing desk, sliding faders to show how he blended the various voices and melody lines that we hear in the song's dazzling polyphonic opening. Five different voices singing five distinct melodies from *Woodcut* are perfectly arranged across the

---

[34] Former Big Big Train guitarists Dave Foster and, earlier, Dave Gregory.

[35] *The Nuno Bettencourt Interview* on Rick Beato's YouTube channel, May 2023.

stereo field, panning from right to left, to harmonise and yet remain distinctive. At any moment, you can focus on a single melody line or singer and clearly identify who is performing.

The current line-up of Big Big Train has become renowned for its almost choir-like ability to harmonise, as anyone who has witnessed the band live will be aware.

> *"Without wanting to sound big-headed, I'm still impressed at the daring of just going out and performing a song like* Miramare *without any kind of pitch reference,"* says Oskar Holldorff. *"I remember suggesting that we used a pitch note in our ears to keep us together, but then we just went out and did it, like at Loreley*[36] *when it was the opening number of the set. I've never been in a band that was comfortable with doing that kind of high-wire act before."*

That this works is also due to what Alberto Bravin calls "genius writing" by Clare Lindley, who had the unenviable task of aligning all of these words and syllables so that they follow their own rhythms but still converge at various points within the arrangement. Amidst so many other album highlights, the sheer degree of difficulty involved in creating such vocal pyrotechnics almost becomes lost in the cascade of wait-for-it moments, but listen closely, and the likelihood of *Dreams In Black And White* becoming a classic moment on a classic album quickly becomes clear.

Of course, the dominant motif in *Dreams In Black And White* is derived from the volcanic bass riff that characterised the presence of supernatural forces in *Albion Press*. The devils are back, but now they appear pitiful and shrunken; the once-riotous, bacchanalian frenzy is stripped bare on glockenspiel before the song's climax is illuminated by another epic moment from Sjöblom.

[36] Big Big Train closed the last evening of the Night Of The Prog festival in Loreley, Germany, on 21 July 2024. Coincidentally, this was the 17th and final edition of the event. The song *Miramare*, from the album *The Likes Of Us*, which was the opening number of the Loreley set, begins with a five-part acapella chorus.

As the colours fade, and everything that was familiar disappears, we sense that The Artist may be fading as well. Perhaps he's gone too far, and it would be easier just to give up. Hopeful strings swirl back into the mix, as if all of Arcadia is rooting for him to pull out of the slump, and the song ends with some delicate, querying piano chords that suggest he is teetering on the edge.

> *"There's an interesting story about the title of* Dreams In Black And White," reveals Clare Lindley. *"Our trumpet player Paul Mitchell is very colour blind, and just happened to mention on tour one day, 'Oh, I only dream in black and white.' And he was so matter-of-fact about it, but I think my jaw dropped. It's such an evocative and poignant thought for those of us who do discern colours. So, I said to him, 'Do you mind if I write that down?' because I had a premonition it would be something I could use in the lyrics. And as a title, at this point, not only does it encapsulate what's going on in the story as Arcadia disappears, but it also fits in with the very idea of woodcut illustration being a process where you literally carve lines, the white light, into the black darkness of the wood."*

> *"I didn't mind being the inspiration for a song title,"* says Paul Mitchell with a smile. *"I've always been colour blind, so dreaming in black and white – at least the dreams I remember – is something I take for granted. During the tour, Clare always had her notebook handy so she could jot something down if she heard or saw something that might be useful for a lyric. It's kind of flattering to have been her inspiration."*

Not so long ago, I read a post on an online forum where a prog fan stated that while they admired Big Big Train's musicianship, they felt the band's songwriting had become somewhat predictable. According to the author, the band needed to take more creative risks, experiment with their sound, and make new albums more progressive. Well, if you are reading this book and recognise yourself as the person with those sentiments, I hope you will agree that Big Big Train has more than risen to the challenge on *Woodcut*, never more so than on the wild and glorious pursuit that is the instrumental *Cut And Run*. Oskar Holldorff certainly thinks so.

> *"I used to call* Cut And Run *'Here Be Dragons' as a note to myself that I really needed to rehearse this one because it's so difficult!"*

More than any other song on the album, *Cut And Run* demonstrates the abundance of creativity contained within this band and their willingness to take no prisoners when they deploy it. Rikard Sjöblom certainly thinks so.

> *"On* Cut And Run, *I do a little sweep guitar, which is a technique I don't normally use. There are obviously many guitarists for whom it comes easily, but I've never had the patience or natural dexterity to play that style smoothly. However, there's a synth melody I thought would be cool to shadow with some sweep, so I gave it a go, and I think it turned out well. It's something I'll need to work on when we come to play it live though!"*

The whole song is such a giddy helter-skelter that, like Sjöblom's guitar, it sweeps you along. The effect is like watching a scene in an action movie where the hero is chased across a skyline of upswept roofs and neon signs by an inexhaustible army of men in black (or a dragon!).

One moment, we're being shaken and stirred by some thoroughly licensed-to-thrill bass pedals; the next, we're dodging stabs of Hammond organ and exploding guitar shells that sound like Duane Eddy playing the melody from *Dreams In Black And White* in the key of manic hysteria. Eventually, it all breaks apart into a discordant *Day In The Life* cacophony launched skywards by a gleefully wicked *Misirlou* surf rock groove.

Ominously, like a helicopter gunship dropping into shot during the chase down the mountainside, the riff of bass riffs returns in spades, wilder and more menacing than ever; the monsters are back and they mean business. Keyboard arpeggios play like searchlights above the rhythm section, hinting at something on a knife-edge – these demons are not about to let their prey escape that easily – and the song reaches its climax in a sweat-soaked, down-to-the-last-bullet finale that at times sounds like the James Bond theme's evil twin played by the Jimmy Smith Band. And it could have been even more full-on, as Gregory Spawton reveals.

> *"NDV is brilliant at writing instrumentals, such as* Apollo, *for example, which has become a kind of signature track for us when we play live. He came up with* Cut And Run, *which we were thrilled by. Alberto then took the demo and worked out ways to bring back some of the themes by using different keys or changing chords. And it became this mini-epic that feels longer than it is simply because there's so much going on. If I recall correctly, there were even more references in there that we removed because we felt we might be overdoing things."*

When I put this to NDV, the drummer let out one of his characteristic laughs and nodded his agreement.

> *"Well, for the longest time, I was calling it* Son Of Apollo *because I definitely wanted it to feel a little over the top, in the way* Apollo *did when I first presented that song. The idea was to push the boundaries a little, to take the band into new instrumental territory. Of course, everyone in the group can play anything you throw at them, but this was about raising the bar, showing what a band of incredible musicians could do if we really let loose. Writing these kinds of instrumentals has always been a great outlet for me, whether it was* Apollo *or other pieces, such as* Bats In The Belfry. *It's a chance to stretch out and give us all something challenging and fun to play.*

> *"I must confess that I didn't originally write* Cut And Run *for* Woodcut. *It began with me just experimenting with a few ideas. The middle section came from something completely off-the-wall – a drum product demo I once did at Sweetwater! I had four kits set up, and while filming and moving between them, I stumbled upon this amazing groove, which I thought I'd better remember in case it came in useful one day! So, the demo was already quite full-on, and the only major change was when Alberto reworked the melodies to weave them into the final version of the song on* Woodcut. *He did a brilliant job of reshaping those themes so they came in and out naturally, and that made the piece even stronger by firmly locking it into place within the record."*

I think it's a great achievement to have pulled all these ideas together into a single coherent track that fits inside the narrative but avoids being pulled apart by its own energy. If you're going to dramatise escaping from the clutches of demons, you'll need to go all in – I mean, you can't 'sort of' escape from the underworld – so the fireworks make absolute sense. As in the finale to The Doobie Brothers' *I Cheat The Hangman*, which makes a run for the hills in its own riotous melange of brass and bass, the instrumental overload of *Cut And Run* is where The Artist may have found the strength to cheat the gallows erected by his demons. On another Big Big Train album, *Cut And Run* would stand out like a sore thumb. But here, it just works despite all its Raygun Gothic pyrotechnics because it remains rooted in musical themes and motifs familiar throughout *Woodcut*.

Using just available light. Winding down around the campfire after a long day in the studio, 28 April 2025. History does not record whether or not marshmallows were toasted.

More tales from the campfire

For when you're on fire in the studio

The Big Big Train express with a full head of steam, Sweetwater Studios on 30 April 2025

Rhodes

Full band performance
at Sweetwater Studios
on 30 April 2025

Oskar Holldorff in the studio, 30 April 2025

Alberto soaring on vocals, accompanied by Rikard on the 12-string electric guitar at Sweetwater Studios on 30 April 2025

Big Big Train and recording engineer, Jason Peets, at Sweetwater Studios, 30 April 2025

A timeless classic. The Wurlitzer electronic piano.

Demob happy. Clare Lindley on the final day at Sweetwater, 30 April 2025.

Mission accomplished (for now) on the final day at Sweetwater Studios, 30 April 2025

Keep moving on. Big Big Train in the control room at Sweetwater Studios after wrapping up a week of recording before heading back to Europe for the Gouveia Art Rock festival performance on 4 May 2025.

Saying goodbye to Sweetwater Studios, 1 May 2025

Pro Tools configuration displaying some of the 400 tracks deployed on the album, as Alberto Bravin waits in the booth at Aubitt Studios, 3 July 2025

Brian Mullan recording cello for *Woodcut* at Aubitt Studios on 5 July 2025

Clare Lindley, Alberto Bravin and Rob Aubrey in the control room at Aubitt Studios, watching Brian Mullan recording cello on 5 July 2025

Clare Lindley recording vocals for *The Sharpest Blade* at Aubitt Studios on 5 July 2025

Spot the difference. In these photos, Gregory Spawton alternates between the Guild 12-string and the Breedlove 12-string acoustic guitars to record *Counting Stars* at Aubitt Studios in July 2025. He explains:

"On Counting Stars, *there are two 12-string parts playing at the same time and I wanted each of them to have a distinctive sound, hence using two different guitars for the final arrangement."*

Maddie Wegg recording alto flute for *Arcadia*, 7 July 2025

An intense performance by Alberto Bravin during the recording of vocals for *Counting Stars* at Aubitt Studios, 7 July 2025. The power and emotion required for the album's denouement provided Bravin with perhaps his greatest career challenge to date, and one that looks certain to become part of Big Big Train legend.

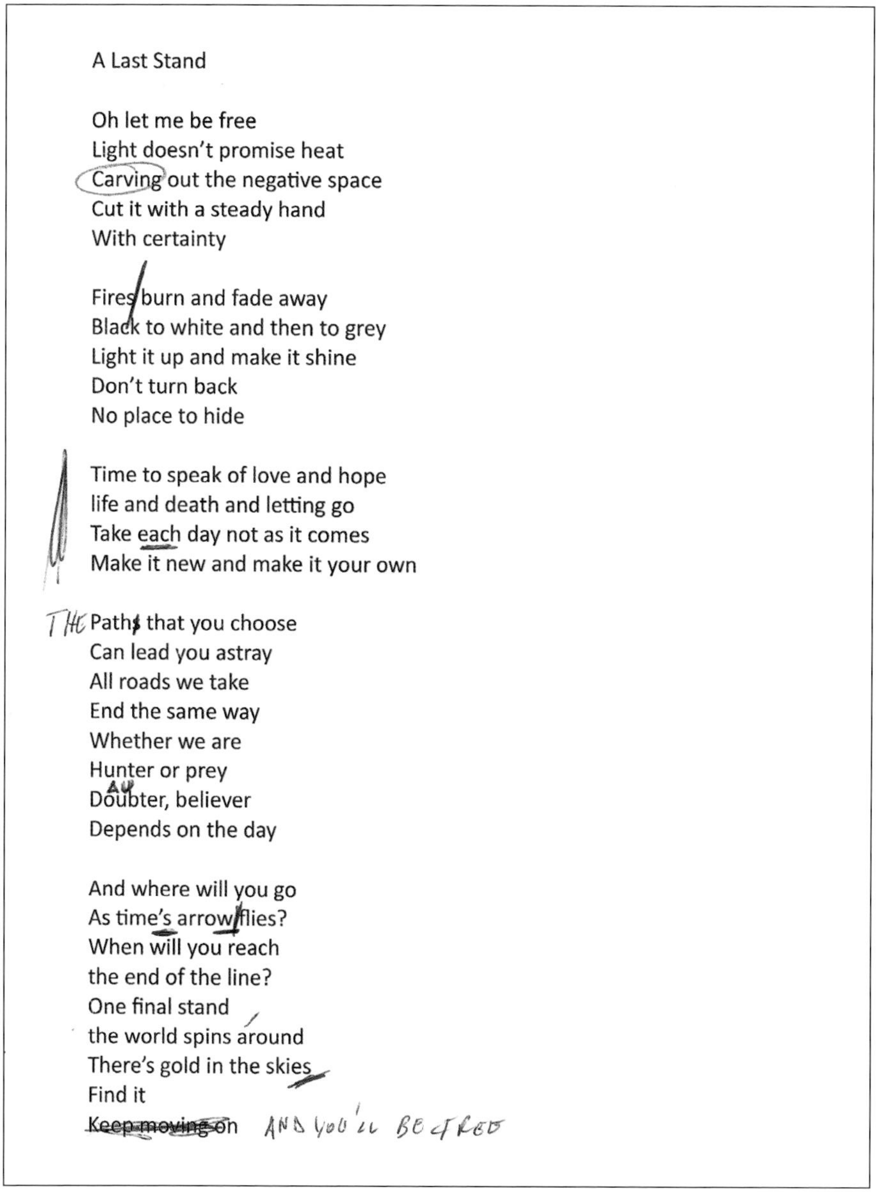
A Last Stand

Oh let me be free
Light doesn't promise heat
Carving out the negative space
Cut it with a steady hand
With certainty

Fires burn and fade away
Black to white and then to grey
Light it up and make it shine
Don't turn back
No place to hide

Time to speak of love and hope
life and death and letting go
Take each day not as it comes
Make it new and make it your own

Paths that you choose
Can lead you astray
All roads we take
End the same way
Whether we are
Hunter or prey
Doubter, believer
Depends on the day

And where will you go
As time's arrow flies?
When will you reach
the end of the line?
One final stand
the world spins around
There's gold in the skies
Find it
~~Keep moving on~~

Alberto Bravin's studio lyric sheet from the *Counting Stars* and *Last Stand* vocal sessions at Aubitt Studios in July 2025. Note the final, amended line. Bravin wasn't happy with his recording of the original line, and after consultation with songwriter Gregory Spawton, the line was altered to read *'And you'll be free'*, which was easier to sing in a high register. The change rankled, however, and the following morning Bravin returned to the studio and delivered a stunning performance of the original *'Keep moving on'* line, which is the triumphant version listeners hear on the final mix.

Paul Mitchell recording trumpet for *Woodcut* at Aubitt Studios, 7 July 2025

Alberto Bravin recording 6-string acoustic guitar for *Woodcut*, Aubitt Studios, 8 July 2025

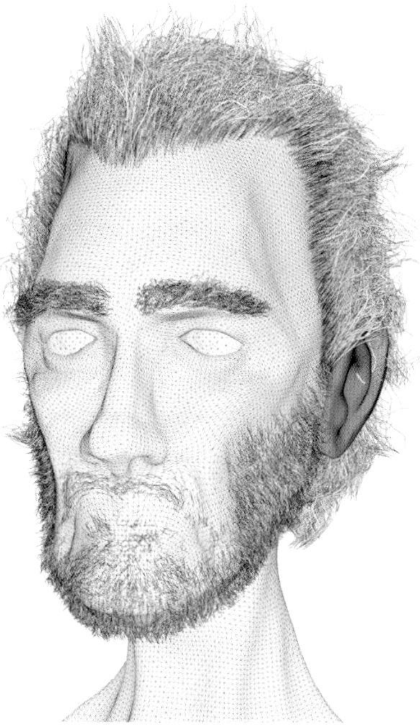

Wireframe of the character of The Artist created by Miles Skarin

Original digital clay render for the character of The Artist created by Miles Skarin

Final textured model for the character of The Artist created by Miles Skarin

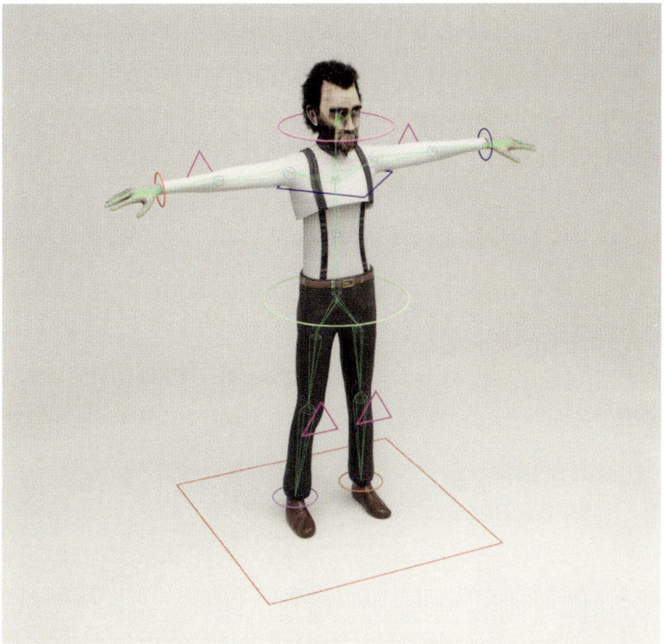

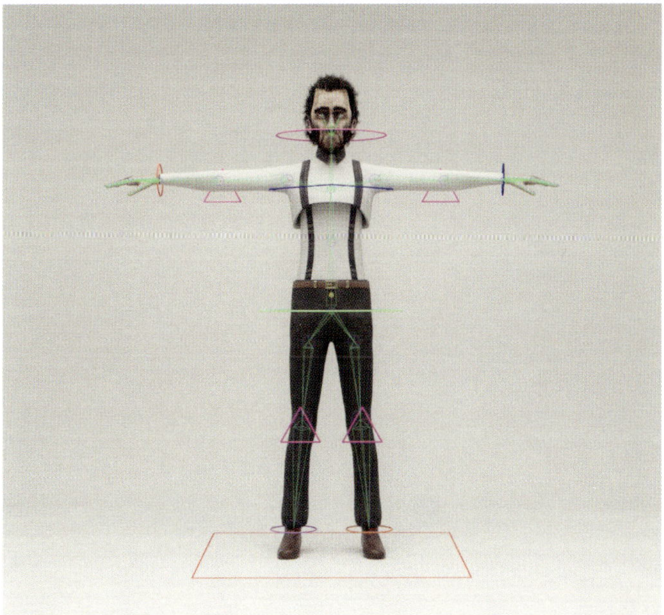

Rig controls from 3D application Cinema 4D showing the different orientations through which the character of The Artist can be manipulated once the basic figure 3D model has been created.

After all of this, both The Artist and the listener need a lie down, which is delivered by a beautiful instrumental piece shaped by Bravin, Sjöblom and Holldorff, *Hawthorn White*, containing snippets of all the themes we've heard so far, almost like a *coda* to the *coda*. The title, *Hawthorn White*, alludes to the fact that The Artist's fate is in the balance, since the scent of hawthorn blossom is traditionally associated with the blurring of boundaries between the human and spirit worlds in folklore.

Finally, the last nine minutes of music on *Woodcut* are devoted to a pair of songs that epitomise the *yin* and *yang* of this wonderful album, distinct yet inseparable from each other. In many ways, I believe *Counting Stars* and *Last Stand* are destined to become Big Big Train's *Supper's Ready* because they bring the album to an epic conclusion, scaling new musical heights while providing The Artist's story with a satisfying, albeit ambiguous, ending.

Counting Stars begins with some heartfelt reflections on the cadence of nature and the seasons, like a scattering of leaves fallen into the sere, set against a plaintive 12-string guitar rendition of the *Arcadia* theme. While these are very much patented Gregory Spawton ideas, in the context of what has gone before, they are meaningful and offer something fresh – as the lyricist himself contends:

> *"My main instinct with* Counting Stars *was that we needed to bring in some kind of philosophical consideration about what it means to live your life well. Because all the way through* Woodcut, *that's been The Artist's dilemma. Has he lived well? Has he made the most of his talent? Has he fulfilled some kind of purpose? And at the end of the album, perhaps some of those questions have been resolved, allowing him to live simply and well. Or perhaps they haven't. We didn't want to make it explicit, so I think the jury can still be out on that one.*
>
> *"But* Counting Stars *is an important piece on the album, and it contains a lot of the elements that we do best. I'm particularly*

proud of the chorus on that song, both lyrically and because I think Alberto's performance is certainly going to make the hairs stand up on the back of people's necks. Watching him record that in the studio was a moment when you felt your bottom lip trembling, for sure."

Effortlessly, the rhythm changes as the acoustic guitar gives way to a *Golden Slumbers*-like piano and Alberto Bravin delivers three incredible versions of the chorus that perfectly guide us towards *Last Stand* and journey's end. The Artist was transfixed by one world, Arcadia, but in a glorious, metaphysical transformation, his consciousness, liberated from all the manic darkness, is purged and set free. Momentarily, he is granted a glimpse of the universal, of stars and distant worlds, like a time-lapse in real time. It's easy to make associations with T.S. Eliot's vision of the universal expressed in *Four Quartets*, but in the context of *Woodcut*, I am more struck by Rainer Maria Rilke's beautiful lines in *The First Elegy*[37].

But listen to the winds breathing,
the unbroken news that takes shape out of silence...
...Strange,
To see all that was once so interconnected
drifting in space

Listen closely to those three versions of the chorus to *Counting Stars*:

Underneath the heavens
Counting stars
And distant worlds
Gleaming like a hint of
Something gold
Set in the earth

---

[37] *The First Elegy* from *The Poetry Of Rilke: Bilingual Edition* by Rainer Maria Rilke, translated and edited by Edward Snow.

The first run-through is beautiful. The second is incredible. The third repetition is nothing short of extraordinary. Each time, the power and intensity of the delivery grow, perfectly matching the needs of the narrative. I mentioned earlier that there are passages on this record I would have loved to hear David Longdon sing, but this moment rightfully belongs to Alberto Bravin. It's his "*She flies!*" and he doesn't just fly, he soars.

> *"I recorded all the songs with full lyrics at home before I travelled to record them properly with Rob,"* says Alberto Bravin. *"I wanted to have an idea where the challenging stuff was going to be, such as those really high notes on* Counting Stars *and* Last Stand. *And there were actually a few instances where I asked Clare or Greg to change some of the lyrics because certain vowels sounded better with my voice on specific notes. For example, it's much easier for me to articulate an E note, instead of an A note, in a high register, when I've really got to deliver a lot of power. And you're always thinking about not going too hard, too soon, when you need to build up to a very dramatic moment. As a vocalist, you have to be aware of the different emotional pitches within a song; otherwise, it just becomes bland, almost brutal. It can't be 100% all the time. I worked very hard trying to get the different levels just right on* Counting Stars, *and I'm very happy with how those choruses sound."*

Momentarily, you could almost miss the entrance of Rikard Sjöblom on guitar, but *Counting Stars* concludes with the most inspirational solo on the album, where all comparisons with Big Big Train guitar landmarks of the past – *The Underfall Yard*, *Victorian Brickwork* or *East Coast Racer* – are entirely justified. This matches, and perhaps surpasses, all of them. Whether or not you agree, I believe we can confidently predict that the finale of *Counting Stars* will coincide with a mysterious dust storm of 'things being caught in eyes' wherever *Woodcut* is performed live.

"There are so many points on the album, I think, that are going to be big moments," observes Rikard Sjöblom. *"And there are some solos, like* Counting Stars *and perhaps* Light Without Heat, *where I think I'll need to play them note for note, because I think audiences will expect to hear those pieces as they were written. Sometimes when you're playing live, you can give yourself more freedom to be creative and mix things up a little, but there are certain tracks – like* Victorian Brickwork *or those two I just mentioned – where the part* is *the part. It's kind of what I was saying earlier when I talked about playing what the song needs. Once it comes to performing live, it's even more important to judge how far – or not – to go. However, it's not like you're putting yourself in a straitjacket by doing that. On the contrary, playing something you know fans are on the edge of their seats waiting to hear is a wonderful feeling when you get the chance to deliver it."*

And amidst so much bravura musicianship, you could be forgiven for overlooking a vocal cameo by the man who, throughout his career, has done more than anyone to move a generation of prog fans to swallow hard and bite their lip. It feels as if the verse he sings is as close as Gregory Spawton has yet come to giving a personal guide for a better life.

Lay bare your heart
Let in the light
And then outrun your fear
Put it out of sight
You can choose any path
But aim for the heights
While you make good your words
Make all you touch seem right

If that is a manifesto, then it's a pretty damn good one if you ask me.

"Those lines spoke to my heart very directly, so while I'm never going to be anyone's lead singer, it was everyone's opinion that I should take those on," explains Spawton. *"I found it very nerve-wracking in that session recording the vocals with Alberto and Rob – it wasn't a one-take exercise, to be honest – so we'll just have to see how it goes live. But I will give it a crack.*

"It's an important song for me. It felt significant to dwell upon some big questions about what makes for a decent life. And I did find something in the ancient poem The Epic of Gilgamesh, *which is one of the oldest pieces of literature to have survived from antiquity. One of its key messages is that we should enjoy life and not go chasing after things we're unlikely to attain. I believe that's a theme throughout The Artist's story in* Woodcut. *It's at the heart of his dilemma, and it's also a very contemporary idea.*

"In today's social media culture, millions of people seem to envy the perfect lives they think everyone else is enjoying, which makes them feel as though their own lives have less meaning. I find it amazing and profound that humans have been grappling with these emotions for centuries, and we're still no closer to resolving them.

"I also delved into Greek philosophy and Epicureanism, which, contrary to popular belief, is not all about self-indulgence, but rather about living a life free from pain and mental disturbance. So, again, these influences were weighing on my mind as I tried to bring the story home in Counting Stars. *Much of this philosophical thinking seems relevant to the last few years of my life. I lost David, which, besides taking my best friend away, also turned my professional ambitions upside-down for a while. And soon afterwards, my stepdad became terminally ill, which was a dreadful time for everyone in my family.*

"Those kinds of experiences, which everyone can relate to, do *make you reflect on the wisdom of being too preconceived about*

how life will unfold and on how best to cope when fate takes you in a different direction. I believe that's embedded in our common humanity, regardless of whether you have faith, or believe in some kind of a universal spirit, or even feel there's nothing out there. Often, the real achievements in life are not the ones that satisfy an ambition, like The Artist's, but are more about how you coped with loss or supported someone through difficult times. Every day is different. Sometimes, it's more than enough just to be there, still standing, which is how I tried to transition between Counting Stars *and the final track,* Last Stand. *I think that's the point The Artist reaches."*

Spawton's profound philosophical reflections were a dramatic change from the ending originally envisaged for the album, but one that the rest of the band were more than happy to go with, as Clare Lindley explains.

"The original plan was that the conclusion would revolve around some kind of twist that would make the listener question whether the piece of heartwood itself was possessed. As if the whole album had been some kind of psychodrama inside The Artist's head, like Shutter Island, *or a horror movie where the camera pans back to the grave and suddenly a hand rises out of the earth.*

"But then Gregory produced this beautiful set of lyrics, and we all just thought 'Yes!' There's no supernatural element to it, but there doesn't need to be. And it's ambiguous to me where The Artist goes from here. 'Keep moving on' *all by itself is a very innocuous statement, but as the tip of this pyramid that we've built over the whole album, it becomes quite profound. It's an aspiration rather than something set in stone. There's still the potential for things to go the other way, for 'time's arrow' to fall short or land in unexpected places.* Last Stand *could mean going down in flames, or it could be the final time The Artist will be put through such trials, because*

he's found a better way to cope with life. And people are free to choose either interpretation."

One insight from behind the scenes is that the concluding line of the album still required one eleventh-hour revision in the studio before it was finalised, as Alberto Bravin explains.

"On Last Stand, *the final line you hear is 'Keep moving on', but when we came to record it in the studio, it was a super difficult note for me to land. It's* very *high, and I wasn't entirely happy with my performance. Because we were under time pressure, we decided to change the lyric to 'And you'll be free', which was a lot easier for me to sing. However, I went to bed that evening feeling less than completely satisfied, which was tough because it's the final line, the ultimate vocal moment on the album. You want to leave the listener with the 'wow' factor. I think Greg wasn't entirely happy either because it was a change to his original intention, which was to bring everything in the story to a fitting climax. So, the next day, after sleeping on it, we returned, and I managed to record the original line as we both wanted. It's going to be challenging to perform it live, but it's the right sentiment for the album. It's less straightforward. More open-ended. I'm very proud of that performance."*

"Alberto has every reason to be proud," says Spawton admiringly. *"Lyric writing requires compromise with the vocalist who has to deliver the words in a musical way, and that's just how it is. Thankfully, however, Alby came into the studio the next morning, determined to have another go at the original closing line and very quickly nailed it. It's another stunning vocal moment by him – one of many on the album."*

Aside from the fact that the tracks segue into each other, it's difficult to separate *Counting Stars* and *Last Stand* because the emotional intensity doesn't diminish between the two songs. Even after Rikard's amazing solo on *Counting Stars* which under all normal circumstances would be the "thank you very much and goodnight" high point, the music and The Artist's journey continue. His consciousness resembles Voyager, travelling at ten miles a second, and there's a rush of ideas and questions. It's no longer clear whether we're listening to the sound of someone falling back to earth and seeing the world hurtle towards them with all its possibilities, or watching them ascend into the universal, letting go and becoming free.

Themes from across the whole album swirl around the listener in an aural kaleidoscope. The world is spinning, but the gold, the so-long sought-after artistic fulfilment, is simultaneously in the skies and set into the earth. Perhaps that's a metaphor for life itself. At times, it's hard to know which way is up and which way is down, and so often in *Woodcut*, The Artist seems unable to reconcile this fundamental truth. Maybe, just maybe, that's the revelation, as the sum of all he has learnt is condensed into that titanic high note from Bravin.

Keep moving on.

And then, in a flickering and abrupt disassembling of Sjöblom's original melody for *The Artist*, there is just silence, as if the ripple effect of different worlds cleaving together has folded into bright air and left no trace of its passing. As Clare Lindley and Gregory Spawton explain, it's an enigmatic ending that has no moral or meaning, no sense of being happy or sad, and it almost stuns you with its suddenness.

It's up to you, the listener, to create your own interpretation. Where will *you* go?

As for me, I think that having waited for so long to create a genuine concept album, the yardstick against which every prog artist is ultimately measured, Big Big Train have followed up the acclaimed *The Likes Of Us* with a record that makes a powerful case to be their finest work to date, even for a band that has such milestones as *The Underfall Yard, English Electric* and *Folklore* in its *palmarès.*

Time will tell, but upon its release, *Woodcut* is a Big Big Train record quite unlike any that came before, and it rises to the top because the concept holding it together is such an assured union of music, storytelling and visual inventiveness. Don't get me wrong, those earlier and much-loved albums have some incredible highlights, but with *Woodcut*, it's the whole lock, stock and two smoking bass pedals that's the draw.

This is a bold verdict, and I'm well aware it creates a critical dilemma. In a cultural landscape that measures artistic value through the sheer brute force of likes and shares, how can one judge in the moment whether any record will have enough staying power to become a classic? Back in 1973, did anyone really know what kind of unit-shifting, bedroom-conquering phenomenon *Dark Side Of The Moon* would turn into? Many may have claimed it was Pink Floyd's greatest achievement, but merely saying it doesn't make it so. And today, it's even harder to grab hindsight from the clutches of the future because we live in an era when every creative endeavour is calibrated by the instant online show of hands that prioritises snap judgements over considered thinking. We used to wait decades for a GOAT; now it seems there's one every week. But still, I will say it more plainly: *Woodcut* is Big Big Train's best album for a number of reasons.

Firstly, for me, a great album will always include a revelatory moment that stops you in your tracks: a riff, a rhythm, a lyric, or a particular way of phrasing that proves irresistible. These are what Rick Beato calls the "wait for moments", and be in no doubt that *Woodcut* overflows with them. My most cherished records – old and new alike – all contain these coordinates of musical bliss, those moments of pure joy and wonderment that serve as a map of my own private universe; a collection of stars whose ordering is uniquely personal and something I couldn't explain if I tried. On that basis, there's a new constellation in the heavens, but I'm optimistic that something may be about to become visible in your skies too.[38]

Great albums turn listening into a full-blown obsession, compelling you to play a record all the way through and start over before the final notes have barely faded. The music that changes lives and suspends time has the ability to capture your thoughts almost anywhere: during a work meeting, in the passport control line, on a bus, buying a sofa or in the waiting room of your local GP. It poses questions that you can become lost thinking about. It demands, no insists, upon your fullest attention.

Woodcut is the kind of record that rewards such concentration. I've been listening to it on the heaviest of rotations for weeks, and it still doesn't feel familiar. On the contrary, every time I press play, I enter prog Arcadia: a world that is complex, virtuoso and richly patterned with time signatures.

On a more personal level, there is just something about this kind of music that moves me, and since you're reading this book, it almost certainly moves you too. For example, though we have many things in common, my partner doesn't 'get' progressive rock. Not at all. What I find dazzling, moving, and awe-inspiring is like a chorus of fingernails scraping down a blackboard to her. I can't explain why we find ourselves on opposite sides of this divide, or what brain chemistry goes into forming the covalent bonds of our musical allegiance, but I wish she could feel the emotion that pours through me when I listen to music like *Woodcut*. It's not so much that "I love it" in a superficial, social media way, all hearts and smileys. It's more like like the full Elizabeth Barrett Browning, "how do I love thee, let me count the ways" kind of thing. Which is to say, the height and depth and breadth my soul can reach. There is no emoji for that.

The U2 singer, Bono, summarised it perfectly when he said:

---

[38] As in the Big Big Train song *The Second Brightest Star*, the ability to see celestial objects "depends on where you are". Nobody ever sees the same galaxy of 'wait for it' moments!

"[Great songs] occupy that space where they own a moment of your life, they own you – you are no longer in control of your emotional life when you hear one of those tunes."[39]

That's what the music we adore does to us. It's what *Woodcut* does to me, and I hope, to you also.

And yet, having fessed up to all of that, I do want to emphasise that *Woodcut* is still a hugely accessible album, to the point that you might reasonably argue its best moments aren't prog rock at all. *The Lie Of The Land* feels like a perfect radio-friendly hit-in-waiting; the joyful choruses in the middle of *Albion Press* conquer the heights of Mount Coldplay, and the beautiful *Light Without Heat* could easily be Heart FM's ballad of the year, even with its brief but perfectly appointed keyboard solo. My point is that the question I raised in the introduction – the sometimes overly anxious "Is it prog?" – seems unnecessary to fret over. Of course, it's prog. But it is so much more. I hope labels don't hinder this majestic music from reaching a wider audience.

"I keep my fingers crossed that people will give Woodcut *the proper time it needs to become lodged in their minds,"* says Gregory Spawton as he sums up his ambitions for the album. *"We live in an era where things seem to hold our attention for briefer periods, so you release an album and two weeks later, there's a clutch of similar music from other artists for audiences to consider. It wasn't like that in the golden age of prog back in the 1970s because there was a lot less music around and fewer competing alternatives like YouTube or Netflix. I hope that people will listen to what we have to say because I believe* Woodcut *will reward them; we strived to make it deep and significant, which, for many, is increasingly a virtue in a culture that can seem superficial. I hope that listeners will immerse themselves and continue to discover new motifs, ideas or connections that capture their attention. It's definitely an*

[39] *Faster Than A Cannonball: 1995 And All That* by Dylan Jones.

evolutionary album for us. It might not be revolutionary for prog as a whole, but it is a departure for Big Big Train and one that we have thoroughly enjoyed making."

And he finishes with a grin that, like the story of The Artist, hints at unfinished business.

"And who knows, we may come back to concept albums again."

Too often, lazy critics dismiss progressive rock as antediluvian bombast, a pantomime horse of a genre that never broke free of its tendency towards self-indulgence or worn-out obsessions with Middle-earth. This accusation of failing to move with the times has always seemed a little bit hypocritical, as if naysayers are unaware their prejudices are just as outdated, mistaking prog rock for something that, paraphrasing Larkin, stopped in 1973 somewhere between the Three-Day Week[40] and Rush's first LP. In reality, the genre is not only surviving but thriving, and on this evidence, Big Big Train are at the forefront of the movement. *Woodcut* is a powerful and thought-provoking contemporary album, one that is rooted in modern concerns about individuality and personal fulfilment, while presenting the band's familiar interests in folklore and fable in a new and brilliant setting.

It's going to be many people's record of the year.

Honestly, it might just be their record of the century, too.

[40] The Three-Day Week was one of several energy-saving measures introduced in the United Kingdom from 1973 to 1974 by the Conservative government. During this period, electricity generation was severely restricted due to industrial action by coal miners and railway workers. The line borrows from Philip Larkin's poem *Annus Mirabilis* – *"Sexual intercourse began / In nineteen sixty-three / (which was rather late for me) / Between the end of the Chatterley ban / And the Beatles' first LP."* Of course, 1973 is sometimes regarded as an *annus mirabilis* for progressive rock because it saw the release of *Dark Side Of The Moon, Selling England By The Pound, Camel, Larks' Tongues In Aspic, Tubular Bells, Tales From Topographic Oceans, Brain Salad Surgery* and *In A Glass House*, amongst others. Quiet year, then!

Album Credits

Inkwell Black

Violin: Clare Lindley
Cello: Brian Mullan
Clarinet: Maddie Wegg

The Artist

Drums: Nick D'Virgilio
Bass: Gregory Spawton
12-string and 6-string Guitars, Electric Guitars: Rikard Sjöblom
Mellotron, Moog: Alberto Bravin
Hammond B3 Organ: Oskar Holldorff and Rikard Sjöblom
Wurlitzer 200, Fender Rhodes 73, Mellotron: Oskar Holldorff
Acoustic Guitar: Alberto Bravin and Rikard Sjöblom
Violin: Clare Lindley
Trumpet: Paul Mitchell
Lead Vocals: Alberto Bravin

The Lie Of The Land

Drums & Percussion: Nick D'Virgilio
Bass: Gregory Spawton
Yamaha C7 Grand Piano, Hammond B3 Organ, Rotary Wurlitzer: Oskar Holldorff
Acoustic Guitar: Alberto Bravin
Mellotron: Alberto Bravin
Electric Guitar: Rikard Sjöblom
Violin: Clare Lindley
Trumpet: Paul Mitchell
Cello: Brian Mullan
Lead Vocals: Alberto Bravin
Backing Vocals: Nick D'Virgilio, Oskar Holldorff, Clare Lindley, Rikard Sjöblom

The Sharpest Blade
Drums & Percussion: Nick D'Virgilio
Bass: Gregory Spawton
12-string Electric Guitar: Nick D'Virgilio
Acoustic Guitar: Clare Lindley
Moog: Alberto Bravin
Violin: Clare Lindley
Electric Guitar: Rikard Sjöblom
Wurlitzer 200, Hammond B3 Organ, Mellotron, Novation Peak Synth
Atmospheres: Oskar Holldorff
Lead Vocals: Clare Lindley, Alberto Bravin
Backing Vocals: Nick D'Virgilio, Oskar Holldorff, Rikard Sjöblom

Albion Press
Drums & Percussion: Nick D'Virgilio
Bass: Gregory Spawton
Electric Guitar: Rikard Sjöblom
Fender Rhodes 73, Yamaha C7 Grand Piano, Hammond B3 Organ: Oskar Holldorff
Mellotron, Glockenspiel, Moog: Alberto Bravin
Acoustic Guitar: Alberto Bravin
Solina String Ensemble: Alberto Bravin
Trumpet: Paul Mitchell
Violin: Clare Lindley
Lead Vocals: Alberto Bravin
Backing Vocals: Nick D'Virgilio, Oskar Holldorff, Clare Lindley, Rikard Sjöblom

Arcadia
Drums & Percussion: Nick D'Virgilio
Bass, Taurus Pedals, 12-string Acoustic Guitar: Gregory Spawton
Violin: Clare Lindley
Cello: Brian Mullan
Fender Rhodes 73, Yamaha C7 Grand Piano, Hammond B3 Organ, Novation Peak Synth Atmospheres: Oskar Holldorff
Alto Flute: Maddie Wegg
Moog, Mellotron, Glockenspiel: Alberto Bravin
Trumpet: Paul Mitchell
Lead Vocals: Alberto Bravin

Second Press
Violin: Clare Lindley
Cello: Brian Mullan

Warp And Weft
Drums & Percussion: Nick D'Virgilio
Bass: Gregory Spawton
Electric Guitar: Rikard Sjöblom
Guitar Pedals Manipulation: Alberto Bravin
Fender Rhodes 73, Hammond B3 Organ: Oskar Holldorff
Violin: Clare Lindley
Mellotron, Moog: Alberto Bravin
Trumpet: Paul Mitchell
Lead Vocals: Nick D'Virgilio
Backing Vocals: Alberto Bravin, Oskar Holldorff, Clare Lindley, Rikard Sjöblom

Chimaera
Drums & Percussion: Nick D'Virgilio
Bass, 12-string Acoustic Guitar: Gregory Spawton
Mellotron, Moog: Alberto Bravin
Electric Guitar: Rikard Sjöblom
Hammond B3 Organ, Yamaha C7 Grand Piano, Mellotron: Oskar Holldorff
Violin: Clare Lindley
Trumpet: Paul Mitchell
Lead Vocals: Alberto Bravin, Oskar Holldorff
Backing Vocals: Nick D'Virgilio, Clare Lindley, Rikard Sjöblom

Dead Point
Drums & Percussion: Nick D'Virgilio
Bass, Taurus Pedals: Gregory Spawton
Electric Guitar: Rikard Sjöblom
Acoustic Guitar: Alberto Bravin
Yamaha C7 Grand Piano, Hammond B3 Organ, Novation Peak Synth
Atmospheres: Oskar Holldorff
Mellotron: Alberto Bravin, Oskar Holldorff
Moog: Alberto Bravin
Violin: Clare Lindley

Lead Vocals: Alberto Bravin, Rikard Sjöblom
Backing Vocals: Nick D'Virgilio, Oskar Holldorff, Clare Lindley

Light Without Heat
Drums & Percussion: Nick D'Virgilio
Bass, Taurus Pedals, 12-string Acoustic Guitar: Gregory Spawton
Electric Guitar: Rikard Sjöblom
Fender Rhodes 73, Novation Peak Synth: Oskar Holldorff
Mellotron: Gregory Spawton
Lead Vocals: Alberto Bravin
Backing Vocals: Nick D'Virgilio, Oskar Holldorff, Clare Lindley, Rikard Sjöblom

Dreams In Black And White
Drums & Percussion: Nick D'Virgilio
Bass, Taurus Pedals, 12-string Acoustic Guitar: Gregory Spawton
Electric Guitar: Rikard Sjöblom
Glockenspiel: Alberto Bravin
Hammond B3 Organ, Yamaha C7 Grand Piano, Rotary Wurlitzer, Toy Piano: Oskar Holldorff
Violin: Clare Lindley
Trumpet: Paul Mitchell
Lead Vocals: Alberto Bravin
Backing Vocals: Alberto Bravin, Nick D'Virgilio, Oskar Holldorff, Clare Lindley, Rikard Sjöblom

Cut And Run
Drums & Percussion: Nick D'Virgilio
Bass, Taurus Pedals, 12-string Acoustic Guitar: Gregory Spawton
Electric Guitar: Rikard Sjöblom, Alberto Bravin
Hammond B3 Organ, Wurlitzer 200, Yamaha C7 Grand Piano, Novation Peak Synth Atmospheres: Oskar Holldorff
Mellotron, Moog: Alberto Bravin
Guitar Solo: Alberto Bravin
Violin: Clare Lindley
Trumpet: Paul Mitchell
Lead Vocals: Nick D'Virgilio

Hawthorn White
Violin: Clare Lindley
Cello: Brian Mullan
Yamaha C7 Grand Piano, Synth Atmospheres, Toy Piano: Oskar Holldorff
Glockenspiel: Alberto Bravin

Counting Stars
Drums & Percussion: Nick D'Virgilio
Bass, Taurus Pedals, 12-string Acoustic Guitar: Gregory Spawton
Electric Guitar: Rikard Sjöblom
Yamaha C7 Grand Piano, Novation Peak Synth Lead & Atmospheres: Oskar Holldorff
Mellotron, Moog: Alberto Bravin
Guitar Solo: Rikard Sjöblom
Violin: Clare Lindley
Trumpet: Paul Mitchell
Lead Vocals: Alberto Bravin, Gregory Spawton
Backing Vocals: Nick D'Virgilio, Oskar Holldorff, Clare Lindley, Rikard Sjöblom

Last Stand
Drums & Percussion: Nick D'Virgilio
Bass: Gregory Spawton
12-string and 6-string Electric Guitar: Rikard Sjöblom
Yamaha C7 Grand Piano, Novation Peak Synth Leads, Hammond B3 Organ, Fender Rhodes 73: Oskar Holldorff
Mellotron: Alberto Bravin
Violin: Clare Lindley
Trumpet: Paul Mitchell
Acoustic Guitar: Alberto Bravin
Lead Vocals: Alberto Bravin, Nick D'Virgilio
Backing Vocals: Oskar Holldorff, Clare Lindley, Rikard Sjöblom

Produced by Alberto Bravin

Recorded at Sweetwater Studios, Fort Wayne, United States in April 2025 and Aubitt Studios, Southampton, England in July 2025

Engineered by Jason Peets at Sweetwater and Rob Aubrey at Aubitt

Mixed in stereo by Rob Aubrey and Alberto Bravin at Aubitt

Mixed in 5.1 and Dolby Atmos by Shawn Dealey at Sweetwater

String arrangements by Clare Lindley, Brian Mullan and Alberto Bravin

Lyrics
and Band Notes

Inkwell Black (Instrumental)
(Music: Spawton / Bravin)

The Artist
(Music: Sjöblom / Bravin; Lyrics: Lindley)

I don't know when it started
This feeling I've a long way to go
Half a lifetime's work
And not that much to show

Searching for perfection
But second-guessing everything
To carve a thousand birds
And never hear them sing

I can imagine the inside out
From darkness the light would come

Cut into the shadows
(To let the light escape)
Who'd have thought creation
Would take so much away?

Never enough
Dreams slowly burned and turned into ash
Go through the motions
Keep showing up
Carve to feel nothing
Work for the silence
Cut for relief
The choice is now
Will I always wonder
If it's the time
To make the connection?
Heart to the hand
Hand to the blade
Dreams manifest
Glory displayed

Searching for a place
Find a different way
Let go of what has gone
And cannot be returned

I never thought
A dream could survive this long in the dark
Like a flame without fuel
It flutters and sparks
And clings on to life
Almost gone
Almost invisible
If I walk away
I'll always wonder
And maybe I'm wrong
To build up the banks
Let in the air
(Take a deep breath)
And watch it breathe into life

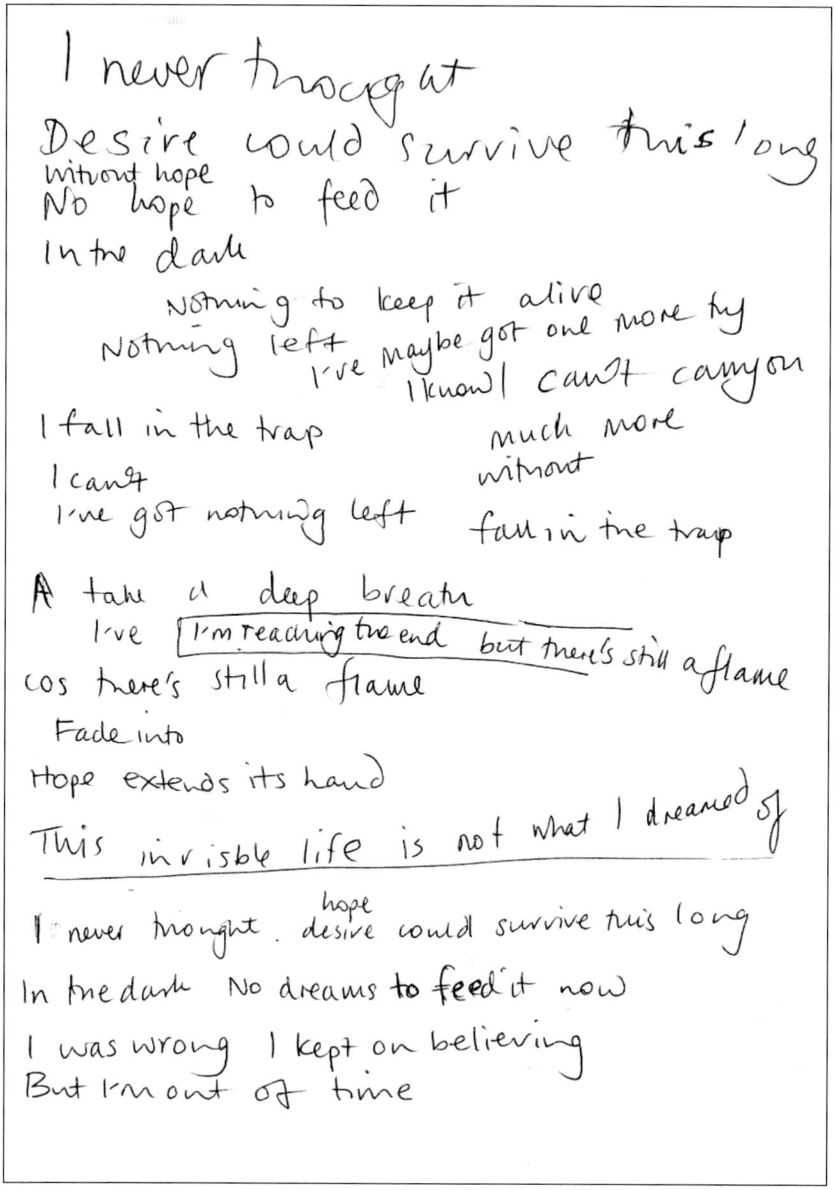
I never thought
Desire could survive this long
without hope
No hope to feed it
In the dark
Nothing to keep it alive
Nothing left
I've maybe got one more try
I know I can't carry on
I fall in the trap
much more
I can't
without
I've got nothing left
fall in the trap
A take a deep breath
I've
I'm reaching the end but there's still a flame
cos there's still a flame
Fade into
Hope extends its hand
This invisible life is not what I dreamed of
I never thought desire could survive this long
hope
In the dark No dreams to feed it now
I was wrong I kept on believing
But I'm out of time

Original notes by Clare Lindley, developing ideas for the lyrics of *The Artist*. In comparison to the final version of the song, it's apparent that many of these thought fragments found their way into the verses and chorus, although, at this stage, they're essentially in a mind map of phrases and free-flowing ideas.

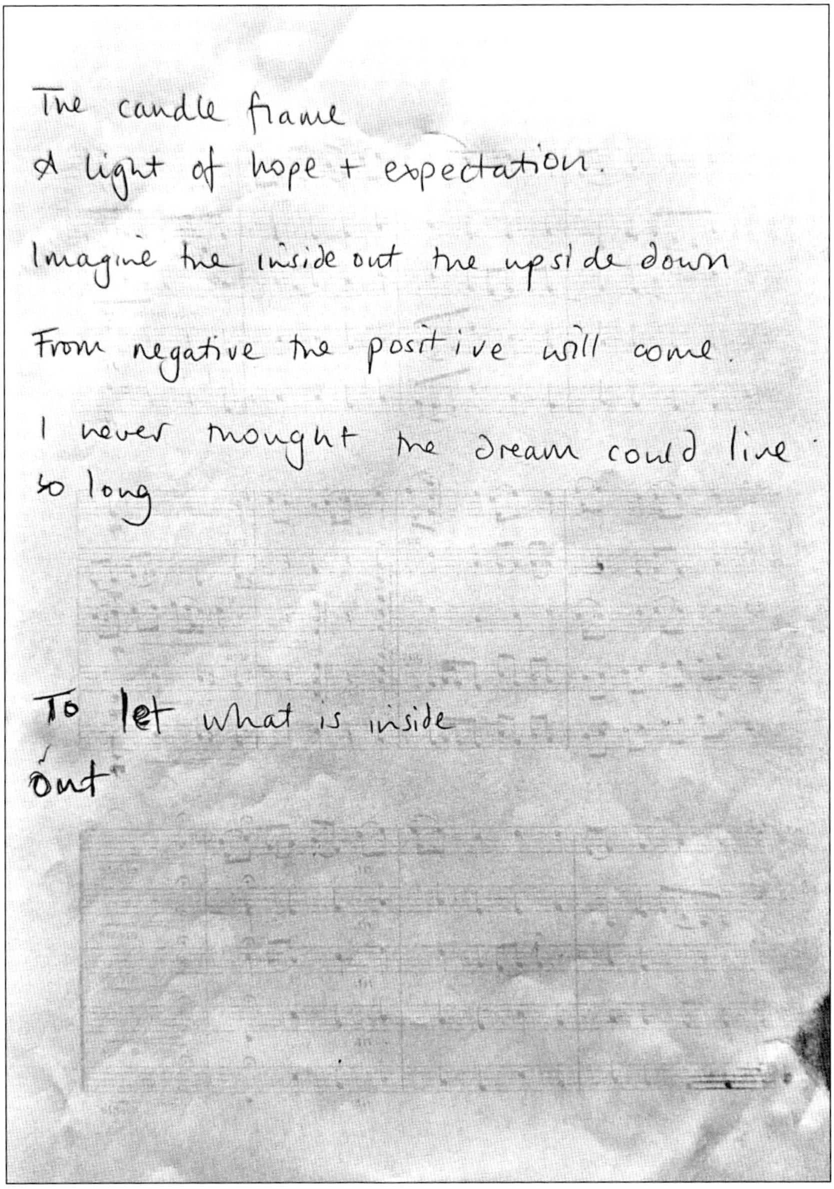

Additional notes by Clare Lindley, for the lyrics of *The Artist* on the reverse side of other sheet music!

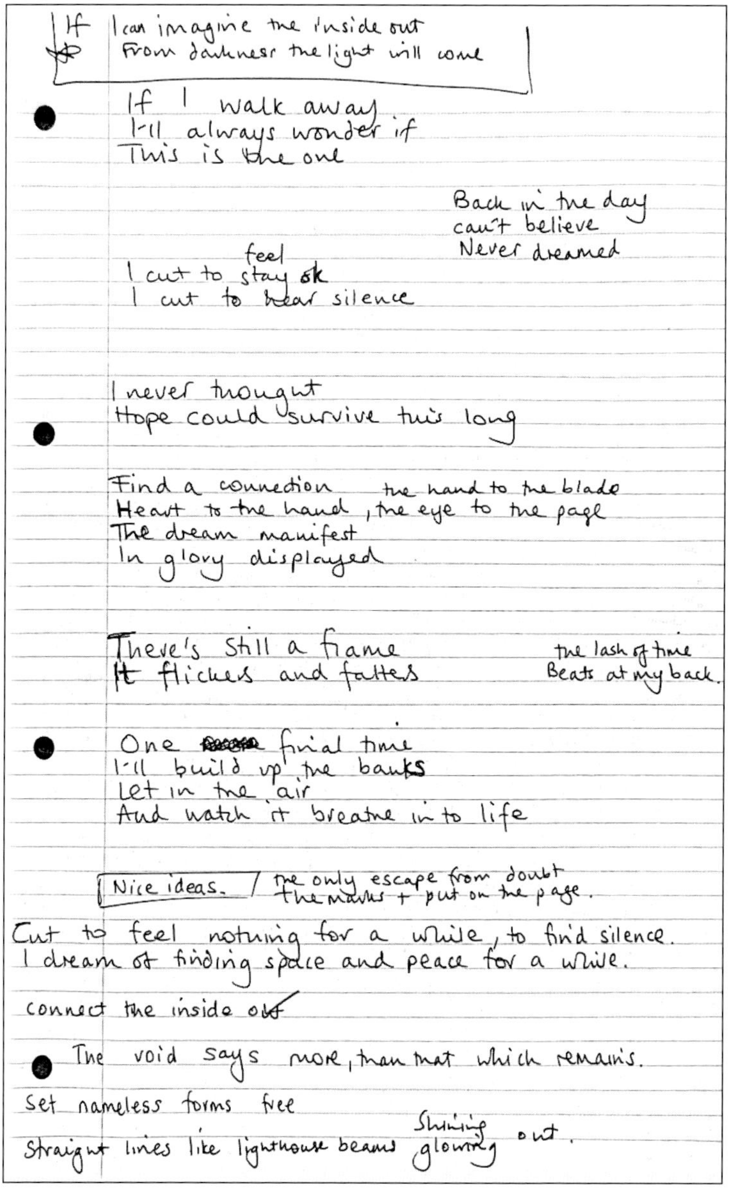
If I can imagine the inside out
From darkness the light will come

If I walk away
I'll always wonder if
This is the one

Back in the day
can't believe
Never dreamed

I cut to ~~stay~~ feel ok
I cut to ~~hear~~ silence

I never thought
Hope could survive this long

Find a connection the hand to the blade
Heart to the hand, the eye to the page
The dream manifest
In glory displayed

There's still a flame
It flickers and falters
the lash of time
Beats at my back.

One ~~[illegible]~~ final time
I'll build up the banks
Let in the air
And watch it breathe in to life

Nice ideas. / the only escape from doubt
the marks + put on the page.

Cut to feel nothing for a while, to find silence.
I dream of finding space and peace for a while.

connect the inside out

The void says more, than that which remains.

Set nameless forms free

Straight lines like lighthouse beams glowing Shining out.

Original notes by Clare Lindley for *The Artist*. Compared to the earlier, looser outlines, there is more structure and a stronger linkage to the actual lyrics of the final song.

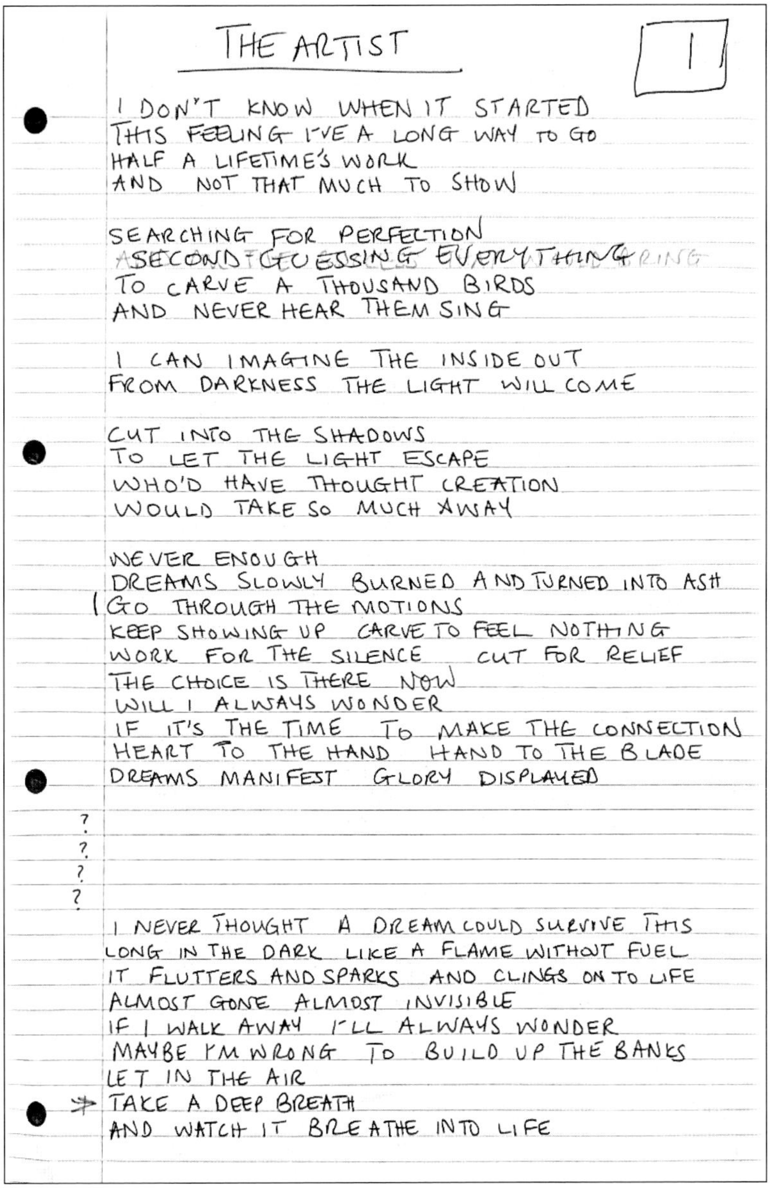

THE ARTIST

1

I DON'T KNOW WHEN IT STARTED
THIS FEELING I'VE A LONG WAY TO GO
HALF A LIFETIME'S WORK
AND NOT THAT MUCH TO SHOW

SEARCHING FOR PERFECTION
SECOND GUESSING EVERYTHING
TO CARVE A THOUSAND BIRDS
AND NEVER HEAR THEM SING

I CAN IMAGINE THE INSIDE OUT
FROM DARKNESS THE LIGHT WILL COME

CUT INTO THE SHADOWS
TO LET THE LIGHT ESCAPE
WHO'D HAVE THOUGHT CREATION
WOULD TAKE SO MUCH AWAY

NEVER ENOUGH
DREAMS SLOWLY BURNED AND TURNED INTO ASH
GO THROUGH THE MOTIONS
KEEP SHOWING UP CARVE TO FEEL NOTHING
WORK FOR THE SILENCE CUT FOR RELIEF
THE CHOICE IS THERE NOW
WILL I ALWAYS WONDER
IF IT'S THE TIME TO MAKE THE CONNECTION
HEART TO THE HAND HAND TO THE BLADE
DREAMS MANIFEST GLORY DISPLAYED

?
?
?
?

I NEVER THOUGHT A DREAM COULD SURVIVE THIS
LONG IN THE DARK LIKE A FLAME WITHOUT FUEL
IT FLUTTERS AND SPARKS AND CLINGS ON TO LIFE
ALMOST GONE ALMOST INVISIBLE
IF I WALK AWAY I'LL ALWAYS WONDER
MAYBE I'M WRONG TO BUILD UP THE BANKS
LET IN THE AIR
TAKE A DEEP BREATH
AND WATCH IT BREATHE INTO LIFE

Clare's almost final handwritten draft of lyrics for *The Artist*. Note the question marks in the margin where the beautifully poignant lines,

Searching for a place
Find a different way
Let go of what has gone
And cannot be returned

remain as yet unwritten in this version.

The Lie Of The Land
(Music: Spawton / Bravin / Sjöblom; Lyrics: Spawton)

Take time
To step outside
A path
That leads somewhere
Far from the city streets

On the hillside
Clings a wood
Where I can
Find a way

The lie of the land
Carries me onward
No place for a man
Under the shroud
I am far out of bounds
The going is hard
I am lost

These broken boughs
Oak, ash and elm
And a deadfall of leaves
Holding me fast
To this place of unease
Birdsong receding

Then, further ahead
Light finds its way
Through the trees
It's all I was searching for
This heartwood is here for me
Though hard and so heavy
The way back home is clear
Sure as an arrow's flight
A burden now made light

The Sharpest Blade
(Music: Lindley / D'Virgilio / Sjöblom; Lyrics: Lindley)

Quiet is the morning's mood
The distant sound of city hum
And river running
Are respite from the voices
That visit through the night

Only use the sharpest of blades
Guided by the steady hand and quiet mind
These fine lines
Are all small cuts
Don't be afraid

Dust motes dance on the sunbeams
Flying airborne and free
But they fade and fall
When shadows come
Just like me

The knife edge seems to know where to go
Every movement perfect
With no resistance
Like someone
Or something
Knows what to do

They say what doesn't kill you
But I say that's just not true
We fold these fragile hurts
And dig them down deep
But they're not gone
They want to be free
And when they come
They cut just as deep
And it just takes longer

Albion Press
(Music: Bravin / Spawton; Lyrics: Lindley)

Step back take an overview
Take in all the scenery
Better than it's ever felt
This could be a masterpiece

And now the time has come
Mix it and roll it out
Press down and hold your breath
Peel back and reveal
Two dimensions into three

Pictures in my mind I've always seen in black and white
I never thought the colours could change
Right before my eyes

More real than reality
Too good to be true
Can't stop, keep coming back
Tuned in to the frequency
Sublime possibility

If I close my eyes and let go I could step in to the scene
A world that feels so perfect
How could it ever be a dream?
And I never thought
I was one step away
Following a whisper on the breeze

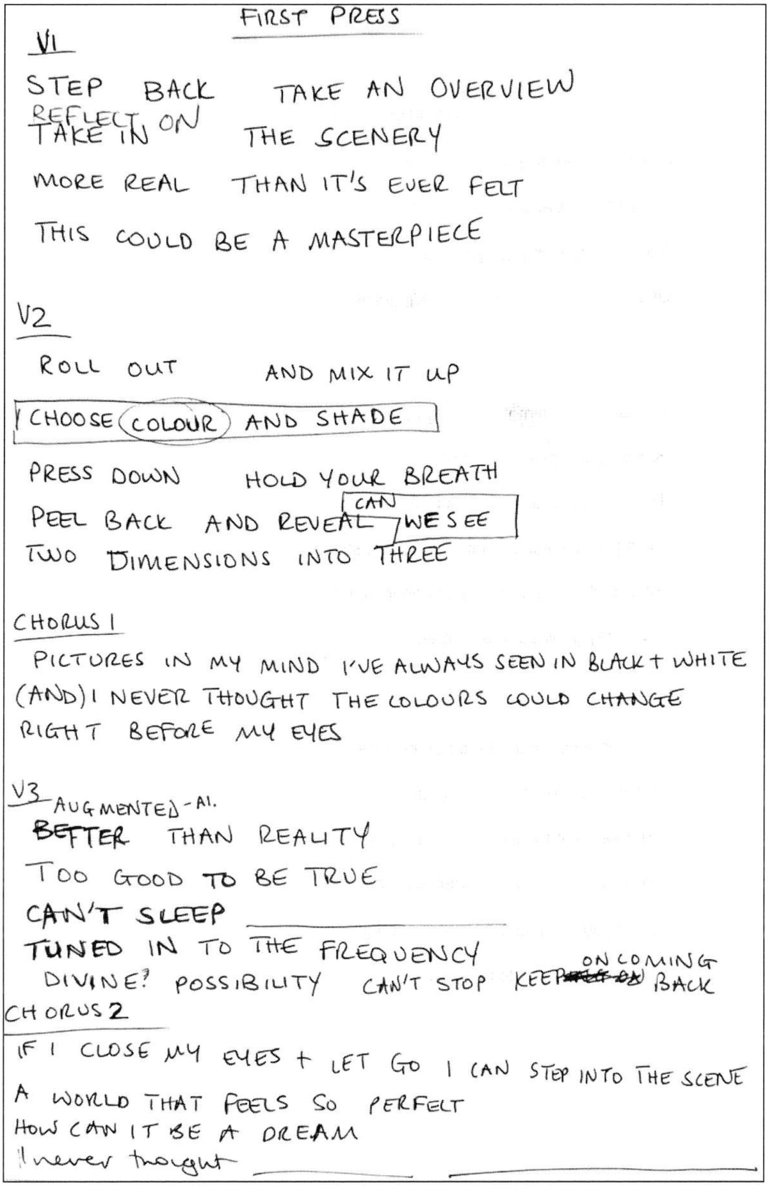
FIRST PRESS

V1

STEP BACK TAKE AN OVERVIEW

REFLECT ON [TAKE IN] THE SCENERY

MORE REAL THAN IT'S EVER FELT

THIS COULD BE A MASTERPIECE

V2

ROLL OUT AND MIX IT UP

CHOOSE (COLOUR) AND SHADE

PRESS DOWN HOLD YOUR BREATH

PEEL BACK AND CAN [REVEAL] WE SEE

TWO DIMENSIONS INTO THREE

CHORUS 1

PICTURES IN MY MIND I'VE ALWAYS SEEN IN BLACK + WHITE

(AND) I NEVER THOUGHT THE COLOURS COULD CHANGE

RIGHT BEFORE MY EYES

V3 AUGMENTED - AI.

BETTER THAN REALITY

TOO GOOD TO BE TRUE

CAN'T SLEEP __________

TUNED IN TO THE FREQUENCY

DIVINE? POSSIBILITY CAN'T STOP KEEP ON COMING BACK

CHORUS 2

IF I CLOSE MY EYES + LET GO I CAN STEP INTO THE SCENE

A WORLD THAT FEELS SO PERFECT

HOW CAN IT BE A DREAM

I never thought __________ __________

Original handwritten lyric notes by Clare Lindley for the track *Albion Press*. The lyrics bear the song's original title *First Press*.

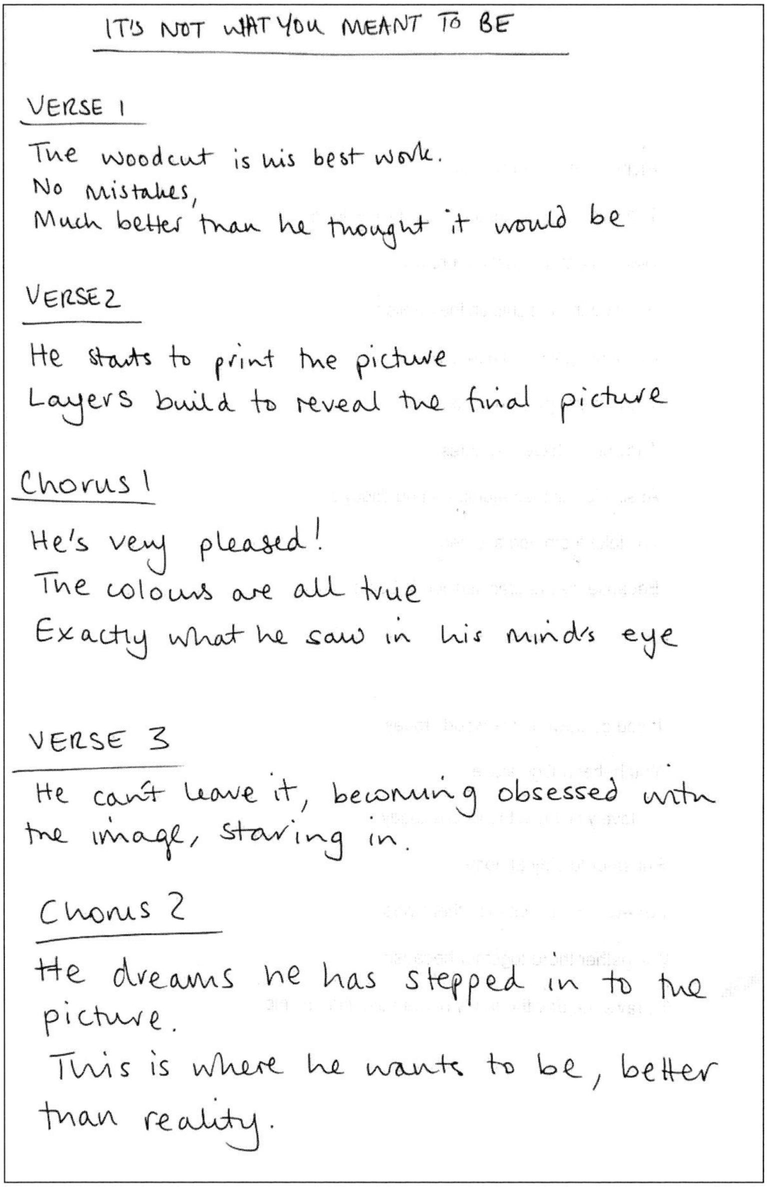

IT'S NOT WHAT YOU MEANT TO BE

VERSE 1

The woodcut is his best work.
No mistakes,
Much better than he thought it would be

VERSE 2

He starts to print the picture
Layers build to reveal the final picture

Chorus 1

He's very pleased!
The colours are all true
Exactly what he saw in his mind's eye

VERSE 3

He can't leave it, becoming obsessed with the image, staring in.

Chorus 2

He dreams he has stepped in to the picture.
This is where he wants to be, better than reality.

Original handwritten lyric notes by Clare Lindley for the track *Albion Press*

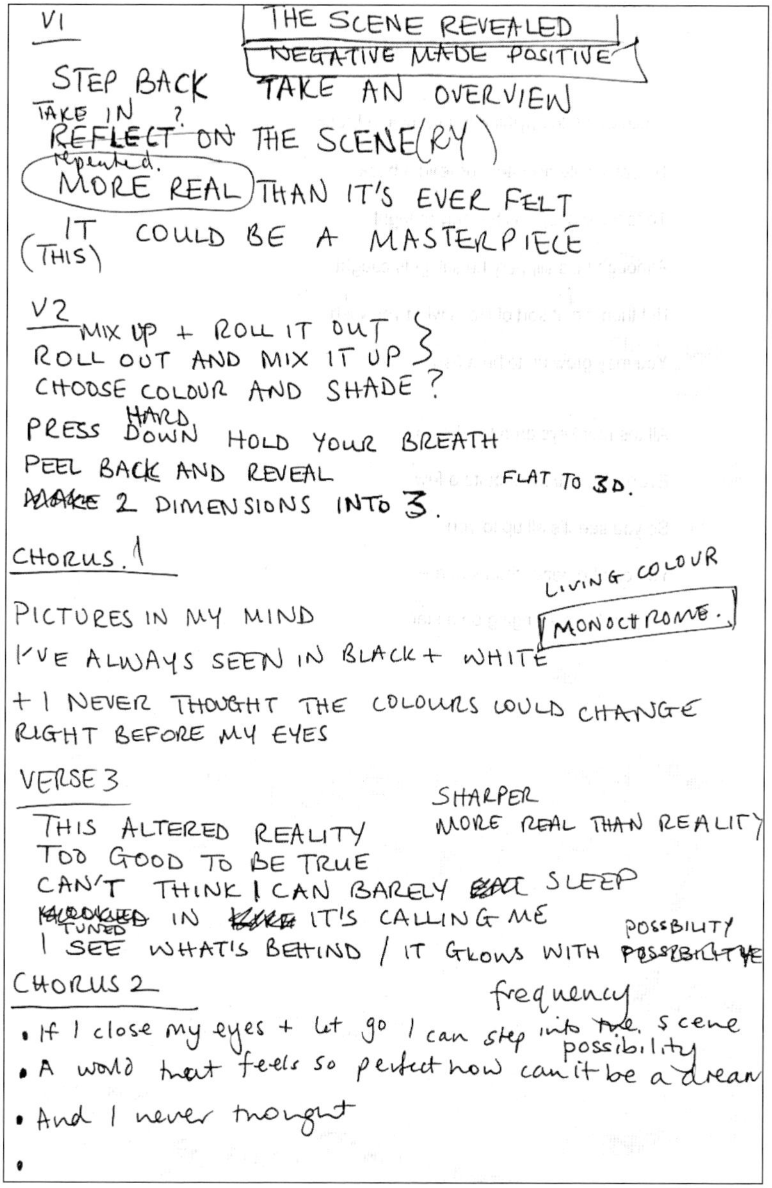

V1

THE SCENE REVEALED

~~NEGATIVE MADE POSITIVE~~

STEP BACK TAKE AN OVERVIEW

TAKE IN ?

~~REFLECT~~ ON THE SCENE(RY)

repeated.

MORE REAL THAN IT'S EVER FELT

IT (THIS) COULD BE A MASTERPIECE

V2

MIX UP + ROLL IT OUT

ROLL OUT AND MIX IT UP

CHOOSE COLOUR AND SHADE ?

PRESS HARD DOWN HOLD YOUR BREATH

PEEL BACK AND REVEAL

~~MAKE~~ 2 DIMENSIONS INTO 3. FLAT TO 3D.

CHORUS. 1

LIVING COLOUR

PICTURES IN MY MIND

I'VE ALWAYS SEEN IN BLACK + WHITE MONOCHROME.

+ I NEVER THOUGHT THE COLOURS COULD CHANGE

RIGHT BEFORE MY EYES

VERSE 3

SHARPER

THIS ALTERED REALITY MORE REAL THAN REALITY

TOO GOOD TO BE TRUE

CAN'T THINK I CAN BARELY ~~EAT~~ SLEEP

~~HOOKED~~ TUNED IN ~~[illegible]~~ IT'S CALLING ME

I SEE WHAT'S BEHIND / IT GLOWS WITH ~~POSSIBILITIES~~ POSSIBILITY

CHORUS 2

frequency

- If I close my eyes + let go I can step into ~~the~~ scene possibility
- A world that feels so perfect how can it be a dream
- And I never thought
-

Original handwritten lyric notes by Clare Lindley for the track *Albion Press*

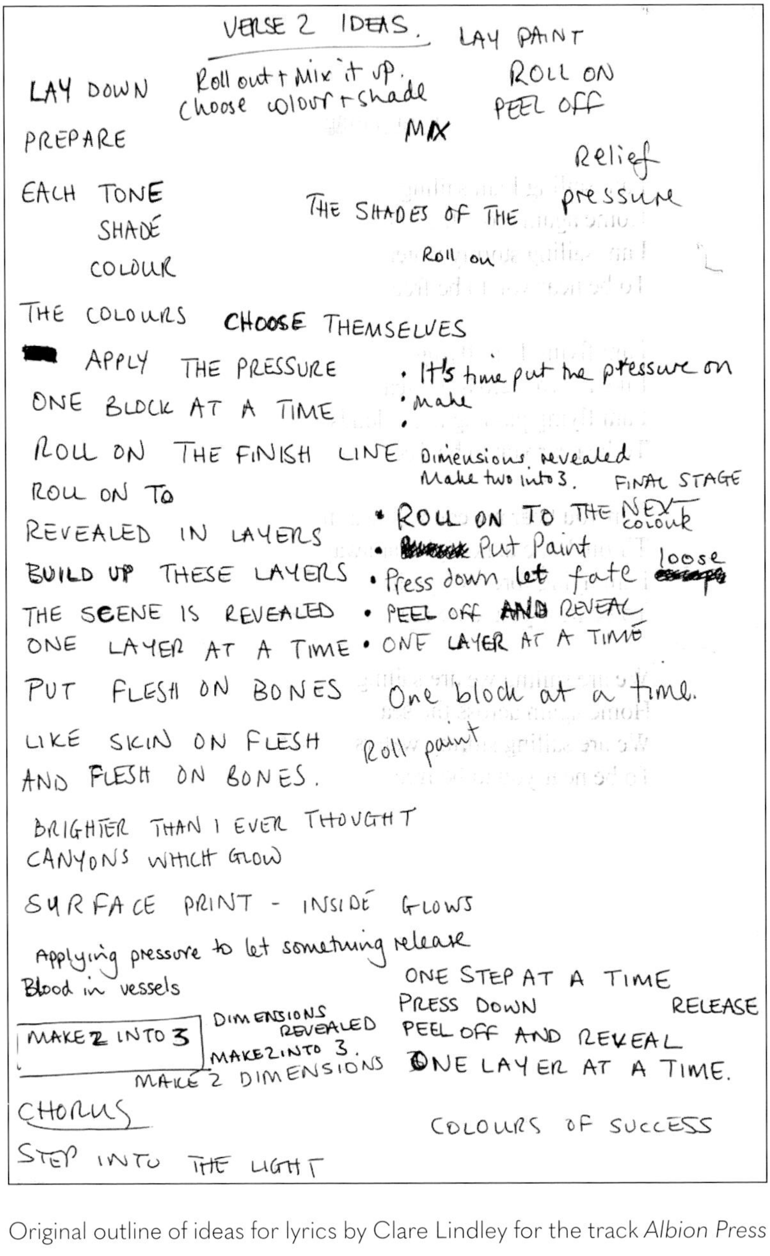

VERSE 2 IDEAS. LAY PAINT
LAY DOWN Roll out + Mix it up. ROLL ON
Choose colour + shade PEEL OFF
PREPARE MIX
Relief
EACH TONE THE SHADES OF THE pressure
SHADE
COLOUR Roll on
THE COLOURS CHOOSE THEMSELVES
APPLY THE PRESSURE • It's time put the pressure on
ONE BLOCK AT A TIME • make
•
ROLL ON THE FINISH LINE Dimensions revealed
Make two into 3. FINAL STAGE
ROLL ON TO
REVEALED IN LAYERS • ROLL ON TO THE NEXT colour
• Put Paint
BUILD UP THESE LAYERS • Press down let fate loose
THE SCENE IS REVEALED • PEEL OFF AND REVEAL
ONE LAYER AT A TIME • ONE LAYER AT A TIME
PUT FLESH ON BONES One block at a time.
LIKE SKIN ON FLESH Roll paint
AND FLESH ON BONES.
BRIGHTER THAN I EVER THOUGHT
CANYONS WHICH GLOW
SURFACE PRINT - INSIDE GLOWS
Applying pressure to let something release
Blood in vessels ONE STEP AT A TIME
PRESS DOWN RELEASE
MAKE 2 INTO 3 DIMENSIONS REVEALED PEEL OFF AND REVEAL
MAKE 2 INTO 3. ONE LAYER AT A TIME.
MAKE 2 DIMENSIONS
CHORUS
COLOURS OF SUCCESS
STEP INTO THE LIGHT

Original outline of ideas for lyrics by Clare Lindley for the track *Albion Press*

Arcadia
(Music: Spawton / Bravin; Lyrics: Spawton)

Morning lights the room
A room which has no walls
A murmur fills my ears
The sound of distant birds
I walk into a world
Shaped by my own hand
Once in inkwell black
Now a spring and summer land

Hawthorn lights the meadow
Bluebells paint the forest
On the wing that flight of birds
Is dancing high above

This heartwood made new land
An Eden yet unfound
A sky lit by sun and moon
Arcadia in full wild bloom

Then the light is fading
And the city hum returns
Shade and shadow aren't the same
Lines once clear are blurred

Woodcut gave me hope
Now I'm cast out and alone
Here beside a fire
Where the flames have flickered out

And inside a storm is raging
High against the world
Steadfast and determined
I will find a way
Will make my way back home

Second Press (Instrumental)
(Music: Bravin / Lindley)

Warp And Weft
(Music and Lyrics: D'Virgilio)

I stare inside – I can't stop
Deep down – I'm tide up in knots
Knife in, carve out, precise, calm down
Each cut – each push of my blade
Finds more of me everyday
Knife in, carve out, precise, low down
Relive each moment in time
Deeper the more that I try
Knife in, carve out, so real, black out

I can't pull myself away
Something stirs beneath the grain
Time stops – how I can't explain
Dig in – the more I go the less of me remains

Where it goes – I can't stop
Can't explain – tied in knots
What's behind – what's inside
(Trapped as I create)
Something's there – I must try

Up and down and I can't stop
Back and forth and I can't stop
In and out and I can't stop
(Trapped as I create)
Round and round and I can't stop

I lose the days – I can't explain
I see it move – I feel it breathe
The more I cut – the more I feel
(Trapped as I create)

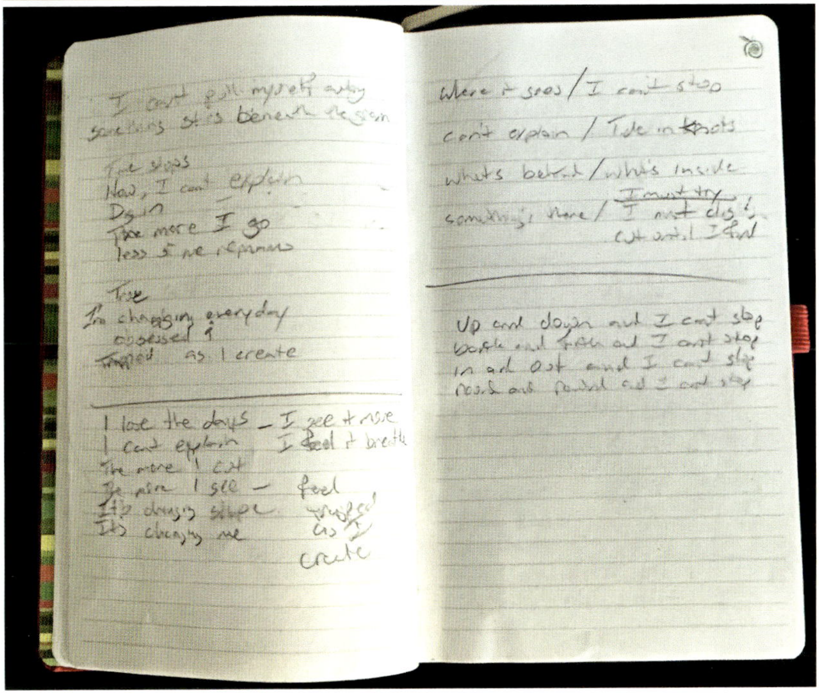

Draft of lyrics for *Warp And Weft* by Nick D'Virgilio

Chimaera
(Music and Lyrics: Spawton)

Let us speak of turning the page
Starting over
Beginning again
Let me show how
I found a new way
With each cut made
I follow the grain

Are we just a flare on a lens
A trick of light in the end
A skimming stone on the water?
The sharpest blade
Has made things real again

Here the warp and weft of each day
Are like milestones along the way
Each path chosen
Each step that I take
Leads me deeper
In this golden place

Are we just a flare on a lens
A trick of light in the end
A glimmer of flame at the field's edge?
The sharpest blade
Has made things real again

Then inside this empty land
Traces bring me back to earth
Whose footsteps made the paths I follow?
Who has tamed the places I have found?

What had seemed a great adventure
Now feels like a dream that's ended
What is real remains uncertain
Where is home?
Where am I meant to be?

Dead Point
(Music: Bravin / Spawton / Sjöblom / D'Virgilio / Lindley / Holldorff; Lyrics: Lindley)

No turning back
I follow the path and see that it leads me
Much further in
The wood seems to wait
Holding its breath
Like it's afraid
If you can't run, you'd better be really still

There in the shade
A dark figure stands, it could be a man
As still as a rock
I can't look away
No breath escapes
A move of his head
He lifts up his gaze
A universe in his eyes

This cannot be real
A figment of my mind
Frightened to look
Can't look away
This is not from my mind made

Caught in between
Two beats of a heart
Held in the dead point
Now I am seen
The cold at the core exposed to the heat
Try to break free
This close to danger is when I feel most alive

How can this be wrong?
A gaze I cannot break
You reach out a hand
What choice do I have?

The walls I have built
Can't keep you out
But stop me from breaking free
(Diving deep)
Abandoning reason made of pure feeling
How can this be wrong?
Why can't this go on and on?

Light Without Heat
(Music: Spawton / Bravin; Lyrics: Lindley / Bravin)

It's not how it's meant to be
The light doesn't carry heat
The leaves don't catch the breeze
The colours don't ring true
I can't ignore the truth

It's not what it seems to be
I don't recognise this dream
Details I could never know
It seemed to be another time
It seemed to be another life
But it seems to be a lie

I'm not where I wanna be
But still it's hard to leave
Home is calling me

Dreams In Black And White
(Music: Bravin / Spawton; Lyrics: Lindley / Bravin / Spawton)

I only dream in black and white
Should not see these colours
Heart thumping, shallow breathing
Pinch myself something isn't right

Open my eyes, I need to
Wake up from lucid dreaming
Running all night
And still I'm nowhere
I cannot find the path
No light to follow

I can't find a way back to the path that leads me home
No place for a man under the shroud
I'm out of bounds

Never enough
Dreams slowly burning and turning to ash
Almost invisible
I never thought
To make could take so much away

All familiar landmarks disappear
Darkness all around, control this fear

It seemed to be another time
It seemed to be another life

Cut And Run (Instrumental)
(Music: D'Virgilio / Dupre / Bravin / Spawton)

Hawthorn White (Instrumental)
(Music: Bravin / Sjöblom / Holldorff)

Counting Stars
(Music: Spawton / Bravin; Lyrics: Spawton)

Dreaming in gold
In gold and in green
Rolling hills and woodland
And places in between
The rain setting in
As autumn follows summer

The order of things
Day turns into night
Earth spinning round and round
From darkness to light
Facing the sky
Watching the sunset
And moonrise

Underneath the heavens
Counting stars
And distant worlds
Gleaming like a hint of
Something gold
Set in the earth

Just out of reach
The hope that remains
But all things turn full circle
And come around again
Winter to spring
Snowfall to sunshine

Underneath the heavens
Counting stars
And distant worlds
Gleaming like a hint of
Something gold
Set in the earth

Lay bare your heart
Let in the light
And then outrun your fear
Put it out of sight
You can choose any path
But aim for the heights
While you make good your words
Make all you touch seem right

Underneath the heavens
Counting stars
And distant worlds
Gleaming like a hint of
Something gold
Set in the earth

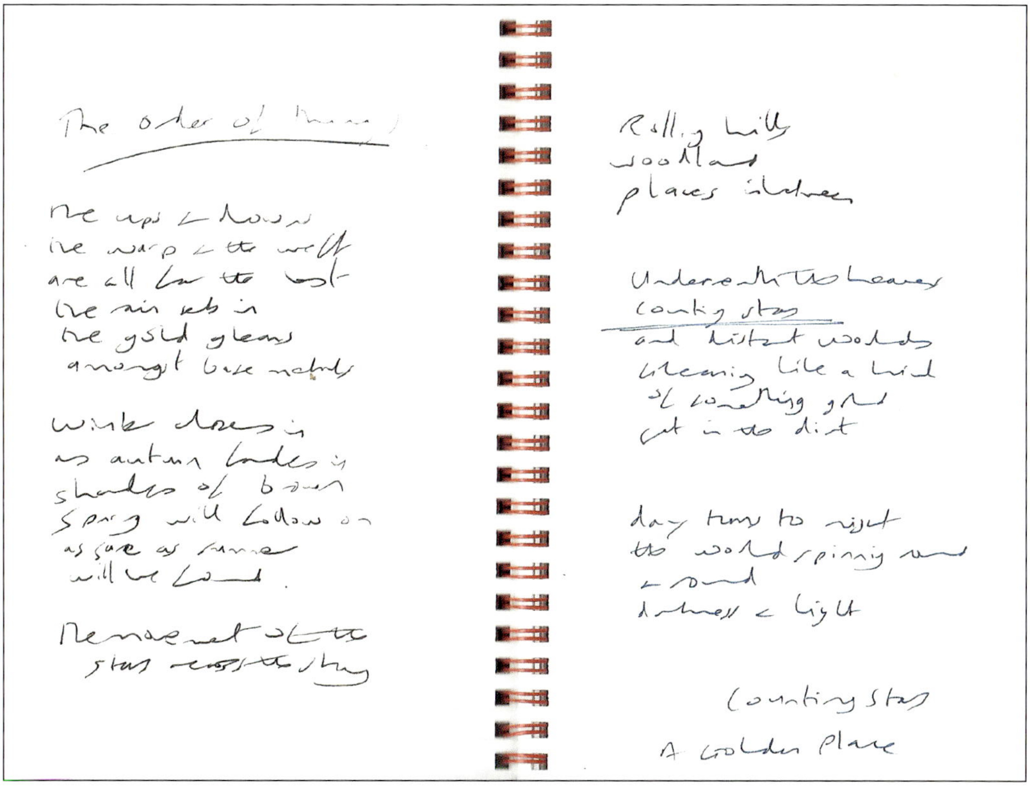

Outline of lyrics and ideas for *Counting Stars* by Gregory Spawton

Last Stand
(Music: Bravin / Sjöblom / Lindley / Spawton; Lyrics: Spawton)

Oh, let me be free
Light doesn't promise heat
Carving out the negative space
Cut it with a steady hand
With certainty

Fires burn and fade away
Black to white and then to grey
Light it up and make it shine
Don't turn back
No place to hide

Time to speak of love and hope
Life and death and letting go
Take each day not as it comes
Make it new and make it your own

The paths that you choose
Can lead you astray
All roads we take
End the same way
Whether we are
Hunter or prey
Doubter, believer
Depends on the day

And where will you go
As time's arrow flies?
When will you reach
The end of the line?
One final stand
The world spins around
There's gold in the skies
Find it
Keep moving on

A.B. Chaos

Assembling the first demo of *Woodcut*

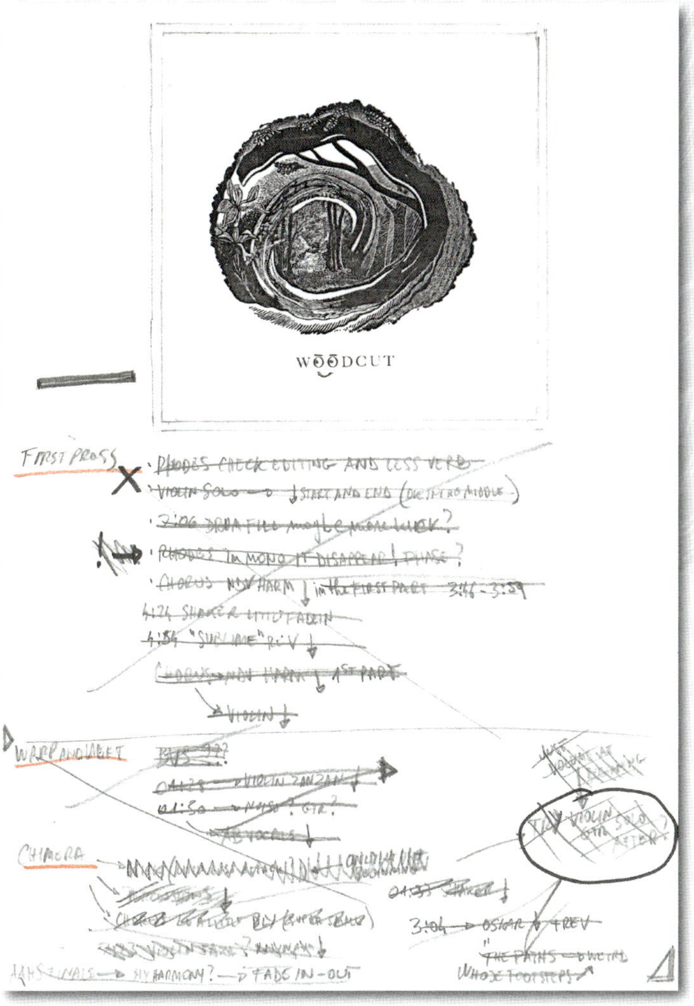

Alberto Bravin's own description of the four month period he spent creating the first full length demo version of *Woodcut*, even as he was finalising the mix for the live album, *Are We Nearly There Yet?*. These handwritten production notes and To Do lists from that period offer a fascinating insight into the passion and incredible attention to detail brought to bear in assembling the first draft of this wonderful record.

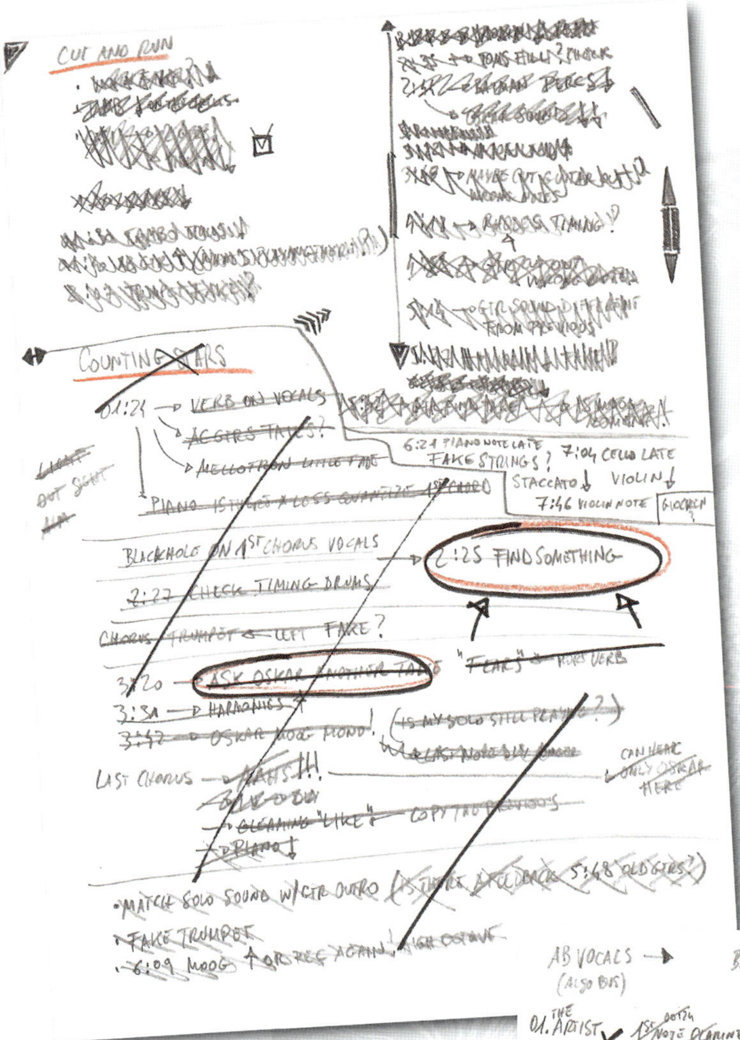
CUT AND RUN
COUNTING STARS
01:24 → VERB ON VOCALS
→ AC GTRS TAKES?
→ MELLOTRON LITTLE FADE
PIANO 1ST ... LESS QUANTIZE 1ST CHORD
6:24 PIANO NOTE LATE
FAKE STRINGS?
7:04 CELLO LATE
STACCATO ↓
VIOLIN ↓
7:46 VIOLIN NOTE
GLOCKEN?
BLACKHOLE ON 1ST CHORUS VOCALS
2:25 FIND SOMETHING
2:27 CHECK TIMING DRUMS
CHORUS TRUMPET ← LEFT FAKE?
3:20 → ASK OSKAR ANOTHER TAKE
"FEARS" ← MORE VERB
3:34 → HARMONIES ↑
3:47 → OSKAR MOOG MONO!
(IS MY SOLO STILL PLAYING?)
LAST CHORUS
COPY FROM PREVIOUS
PIANO ↓
CAN HEAR ONLY OSKAR HERE
•MATCH SOLO SOUND W/GTR OUTRO
5:48 OLD GTRS?
•FAKE TRUMPET
•6:09 MOOG ↑ OR REC AGAIN! HIGH OCTAVE

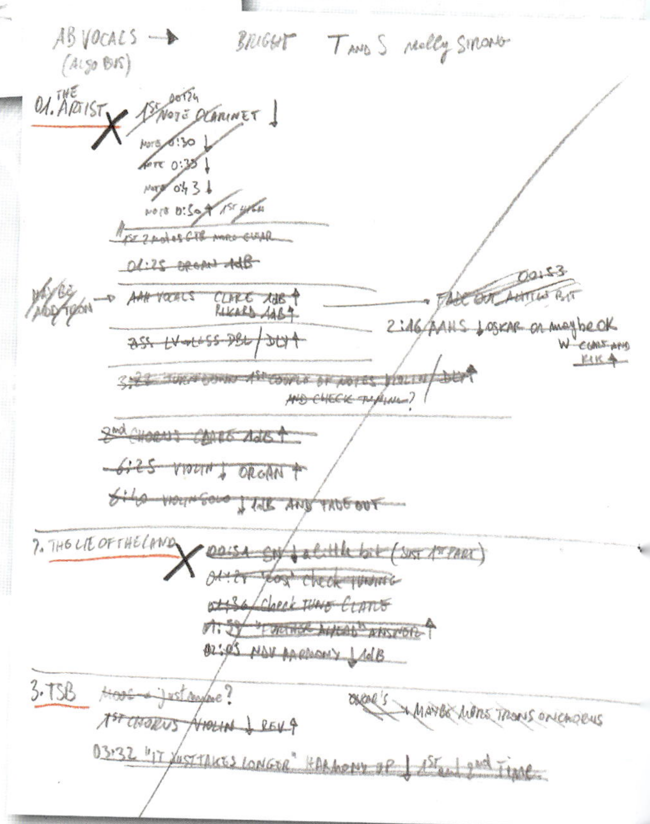
AB VOCALS → BRIGHT T AND S really strong
(ALSO BVS)
01. THE ARTIST
1ST NOTE CLARINET ↓
NOTE 0:30 ↓
NOTE 0:35 ↓
NOTE 0:43 ↓
NOTE 0:50 ↑
01:25 ORGAN 1dB
MAYBE MELLOTRON → AAH VOCALS CLARE 1dB ↑ RIKARD 1dB ↑
FADE OUT
00:53
2:46 AAHS ↓ OSKAR on maybe OK
AND CHECK TIMING?
2ND CHORUS CLARE 1dB ↑
6:25 VIOLIN ↓ ORGAN ↑
8:40 VIOLIN SOLO ↓ 1dB AND FADE OUT
7. THE LIE OF THE LAND
00:54 ... a little bit (JUST 1ST PART)
01:24 'COS' check TIMING
01:36 Check TIME CLARE
02:05 NEW HARMONY ↓ 1dB
3. TSB
MOOG - just maybe?
1ST CHORUS VIOLIN ↓ REV ↑
OSKAR'S → MAYBE MORE TRANS ON CHORUS
03:32 "IT JUST TAKES LONGER" HARMONY UP ↓ 1ST and 2nd Time

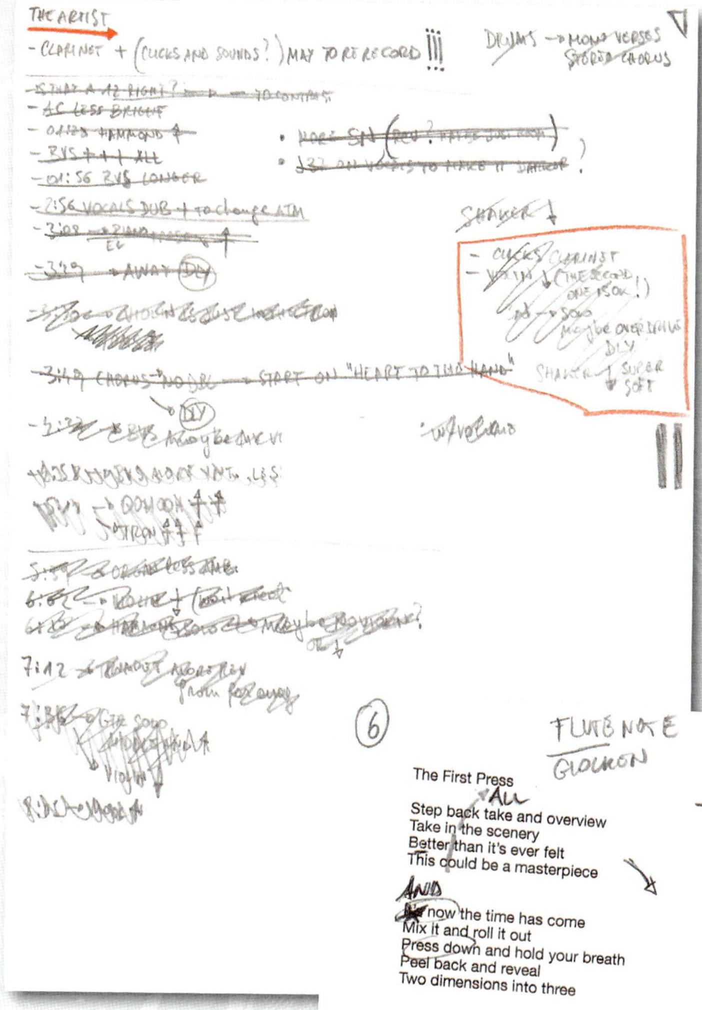

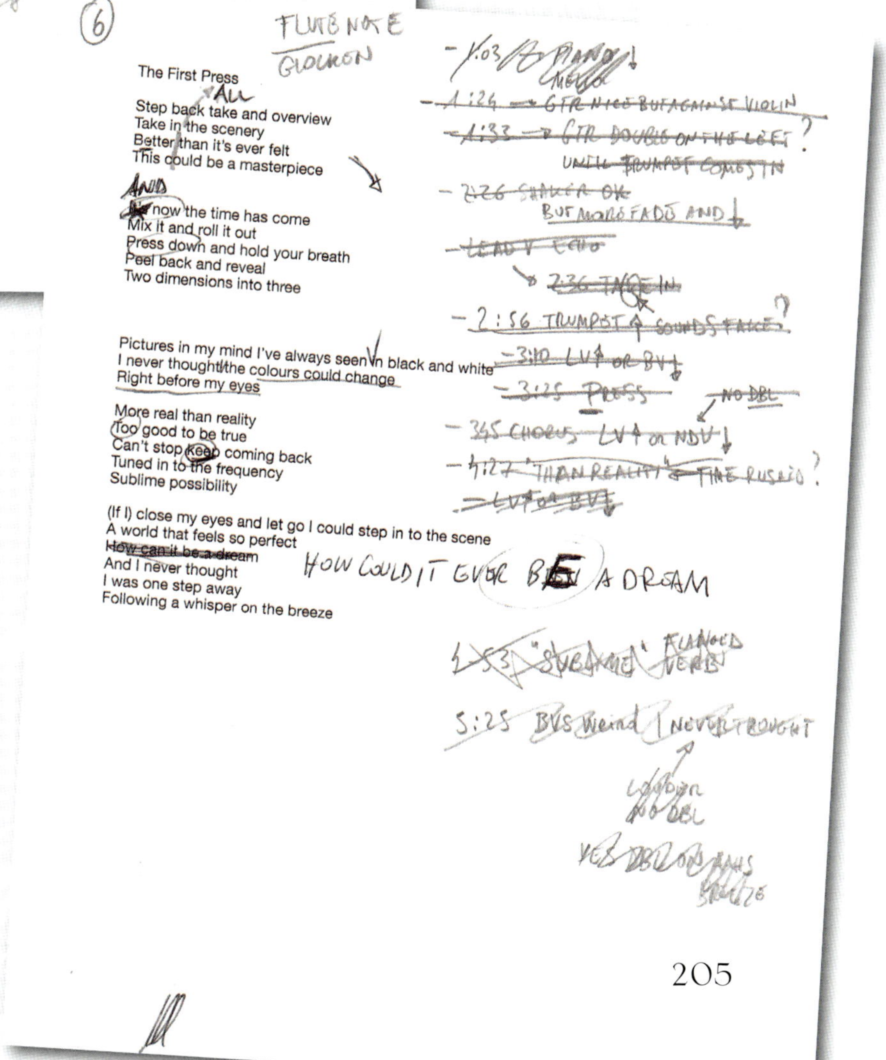

FLUTE NOTE
GLOCKEN

The First Press

ALL
Step back take and overview
Take in the scenery
Better than it's ever felt
This could be a masterpiece

AND
~~It~~ now the time has come
Mix it and roll it out
Press down and hold your breath
Peel back and reveal
Two dimensions into three

Pictures in my mind I've always seen in black and white
I never thought the colours could change
Right before my eyes

More real than reality
Too good to be true
Can't stop keep coming back
Tuned in to the frequency
Sublime possibility

(If I) close my eyes and let go I could step in to the scene
A world that feels so perfect
~~How can it be a dream~~
HOW COULD IT EVER BE A DREAM
And I never thought
I was one step away
Following a whisper on the breeze

ACKNOWLEDGEMENTS

While I haven't, of course, listened to *Woodcut* as deeply and with as much investment as the members of Big Big Train themselves, the album has been a near-constant presence in my life during the three months it took to research and write this book. I'm grateful to Alberto, Clare, Gregory, Nick, Oskar, Paul and Rikard for the privilege of contributing to the album's release and for giving me their time for interviews. Also, to Nick Shilton, of Kingmaker Management, for his kind support, wisdom and sound advice; to the illustrator, Robin Mackenzie, for his fascinating insights into how he made the woodcut for *Woodcut*; to Miles Skarin for sharing how he brought The Artist to life; to the sharp Cambridge eyes of Professor Geoff Parks for proofreading the manuscript and catching all those Oxford typos (but hopefully not too many commas, albeit there were quite a few non-curly apostrophes doing their best to sneak in); to Leo Liu from MUNCH Munchmuseet in Oslo; to the team of Sucre Café in Barcelona for taking such good care of wifinomad authors; to Kevin Moore of KM Digital for once again typesetting and making sense of it all; to my partner, Beth De Ávila, who doesn't really like prog that much but has always been generously forgiving of the fact that I do (thank you, beloved!); to all the Big Big Train and prog fans who thought, 'This looks quite interesting, I'll give it a read.' And finally, to the memory of the inspirational David Longdon, who once sang, 'What do you do, when what you did has gone?' I'm thankful his friends in this wonderful band found the answer to that question. Keep moving on!

A.S.

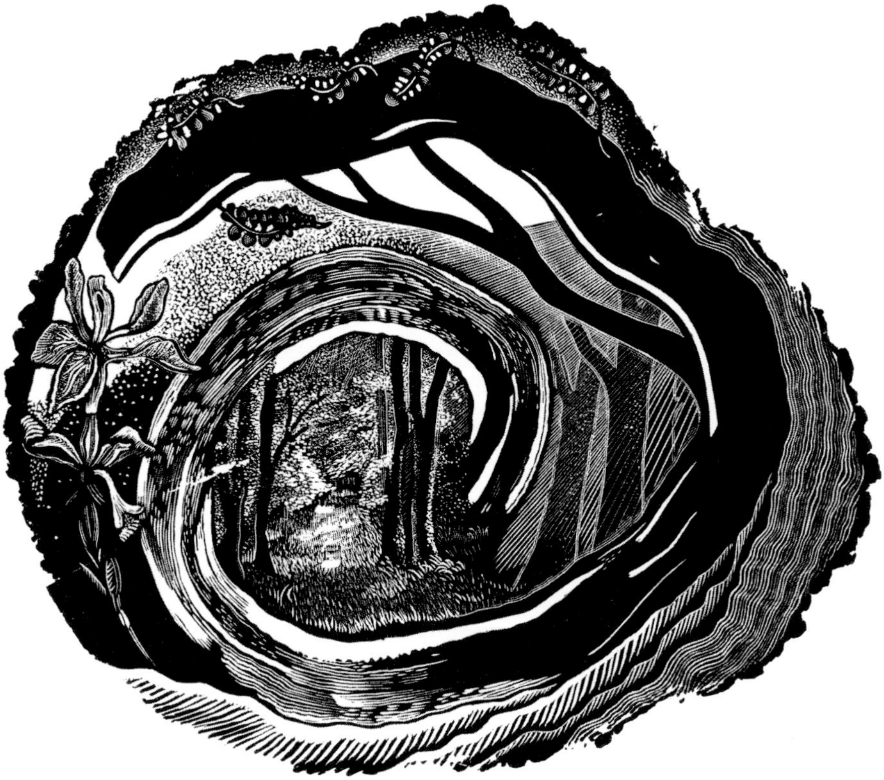